The MANCHESTER CAB MYSTERY

The MANCHESTER CAB MYSTERY

Peter Tomlinson

HALSGROVE

First published in Great Britain in 2022

© 2022, Peter Tomlinson

All rights reserved. No part of this publication may be reproduced, stored in a retrieval system, or transmitted in any form or by any means without the prior permission of the copyright holder.

British Library Cataloguing-in-Publication Data
A CIP record for this title is available from the British Library

ISBN 978 0 85704 360 3

Halsgrove
Halsgrove House,
Ryelands Business Park,
Bagley Road, Wellington, Somerset TA21 9PZ
Tel: 01823 653777   Fax: 01823 216796
email: sales@halsgrove.com

Part of the Halsgrove group of companies
Information on all Halsgrove titles is available at: www.halsgrove.com

Printed and bound in India by Parksons Graphics Ltd

Contents

Acknowledgements 11

Foreword 13

List Of Characters 15

Introduction 19

    The Crime 19

    The Chief Detective Inspector 32

    The Prisoner 36

    Messrs. Robert Fletcher and Son 39

    Victorian Manchester 40

PART ONE: THE JUDICIAL INQUIRY 49

Chapter I	The Coroner's Court, Day One, March 1st	50
Chapter II	The City Police Court, First Appearance, March 2nd	56
Chapter III	The City Police Court, Second Appearance, March 4th	60
Chapter IV	The Coroner's Court, Day Two, March 4th	61
Chapter V	The City Police Court, Third Appearance, March 5th	67
Chapter VI	The Coroner's Court, Day Three, March 5th	68
Chapter VII	The City Police Court, Fourth Appearance, March 7th	73
Chapter VIII	The City Police Court, Fifth Appearance, March 8th	77

PART TWO: THE POLICE INVESTIGATION 83

Chapter IX	The Police Investigation, February 27th 84
Chapter X	The Police Investigation, February 28th 87
Chapter XI	The Police Investigation, March 1st 90
Chapter XII	The Police Investigation, March 2nd 94
Chapter XIII	The Old Market Place, January 8th 96
Chapter XIV	The Police Investigation, March 3rd 101
Chapter XV	The Police Investigation, March 11th and 13th 103

PART THREE: THE TRIAL 105

Chapter XVI	The Trial, Day One, March 18th, The Case for the Prosecution 106
Chapter XVII	The Trial, Day One, March 18th, The Prosecution Witnesses 114
Chapter XVIII	The Trial, Day Two, March 19th, The Medical Evidence 122
Chapter XIX	The Trial, Day Two, March 19th, The Verdict 127

PART FOUR: ANALYSIS OF THE CASE 135

Chapter XX	The Press Commentaries 136
Chapter XXI	The Medical Debate 140
Chapter XXII	Dr Ernest Reynolds' Medical Opinion 146

PART FIVE: CHARLES PARTON'S ACCOUNT ... 149

Chapter XXIII   Introduction ... 150

Chapter XXIV   Charles Parton's Disclosure, Part I ... 151

Chapter XXV   Charles Parton's Disclosure, Part II ... 155

Dedication

This book is dedicated to Marie Wightman and Bernard Tomlinson.

Acknowledgements

To my wife, Kelly Stevenson, for her support during the compilation of this book and for her suggestions on improving the text. Also, for purchasing for me the book *Manchester.... The Sinister Side*, by Steve Jones, through which I was first introduced to the *Manchester Cab Mystery* and Jerome Caminada – the inspiration for this work.

To Sara Lee for her kind permission to reproduce Parton's own account from Chapter 25 of her book *Strange Tales From Strangeways*, published by True Crime Library.

To Steve Jones for lending me his *Illustrated Police News* microfilm from which I obtained additional information on the case and the images used on the jacket.

To Terry Harding, Secretary of the Caminada Society, for his kind permission to use biographical information on Jerome Caminada published on the Society's web site, www.gmpsportsclub.com/CAMINADA.aspx.

To the *Manchester Guardian* for kindly allowing the reproduction of material from their numerous newspaper reports of the case from 1889, 1904 and 1925.

To the *British Medical Journal* for permission to use material from letters and articles around the case published in the journal in 1889.

Foreword

On the morning of Wednesday, February 27th, 1889, the inhabitants of Manchester awoke and were startled to read newspaper articles reporting that on the previous evening a gentleman had been found dead in a "Growler" (four wheel) cab in the heart of the city under mysterious and suspicious circumstances. The situation bore a strong resemblance to that with which the public had just then become familiar in the popular Australian novel, *The Mystery of a Hansom Cab*, written by Fergus Hume and published three years earlier.

This book chronicles the events around this true crime that at the time was termed the "Manchester Cab Mystery." John Fletcher, a successful and wealthy businessman, was found close to death in a cab, in the heart of the city of Manchester, on a cold, 1889 February evening. He died on being conveyed by the police to the Manchester Royal Infirmary. Jerome Caminada, a Chief Detective Inspector in the city's police force, was immediately assigned to the case to determine if Fletcher's death was due to natural causes or if something more sinister had taken place. Within three weeks the alleged culprit, Charles Parton, was arrested and tried for the murder of John Fletcher.

This book came about as a result of a recent visit to Manchester. I was born and bred in Manchester but now live in Toronto. While in Manchester, my wife bought me a book called, *Manchester … The Sinister Side*, by Steve Jones, A Wicked Publication. This book gives an informative and comprehensive account of the living conditions of the working class and the types of crime prevalent in Manchester in the period 1853 to 1914. However, more importantly, this text detailed a "famous" case, the "Manchester Cab Mystery," investigated by a "celebrated" local detective, Jerome Caminada, neither of which I had heard of despite being brought up in the City. Unable to understand how this could be, I was intrigued enough to investigate further. By reading contemporary newspaper reports I uncovered what I consider to be a fascinating, real life mystery investigated by Manchester's own super sleuth.

The work is not intended to be an analysis or critique of the case, but to merely chronicle the events of the case as they would have unfolded in the media at the time before inhabitants of the city, and the country at large. Source documents include the *Manchester Guardian*, the autobiography of Jerome Caminada, articles in the *British Medical Journal* and Charles Parton's own written account. The main portion of the work is divided into five parts. Part One documents the initial judicial inquiry at the Coroner's and City Police Courts in Manchester. Part Two reviews the police investigation and reveals some special techniques employed by Jerome Caminada in identifying, arresting and bringing to justice the accused. Part Three documents the criminal trial at the Liverpool Assizes with the appearance of an important new witness not heard from in the earlier inquiry in Manchester. Part Four analyses the case in terms of newspaper reviews of the trial, together with a debate between medical men exchanged through letters published in the *British Medical Journal* discussing the quality of the forensic evidence. The final part of the book presents Parton's version of the events in his own words and contains a contemporary description of prison conditions. The book offers insights into the workings of the criminal justice system and the level of sophistication of forensic medicine at the time, and spotlights Jerome Caminada, Manchester's most acclaimed detective. In addition, since in those days trials were often recorded verbatim in the newspapers, this work also documents the style of English language in use at the time. The Introduction to the book gives additional information on the crime, the lives of Jerome Caminada and Charles Parton, and the living conditions in the centre of Manchester around the late nineteenth century.

List Of Characters

Name	Involvement
Allinson, William	Detective Sergeant who saw the Prisoner get off the driver's seat and get inside Coleman's cab
Burton, William	Solicitor for the Prisoner at the Coroner's and City Police Courts
Caminada, Jerome	The Chief Detective Inspector
Charles, "Justice"	Judge at the Prisoner's trial at the Liverpool Assizes
Cobbett, William	Solicitor retained by the police to present the evidence against the Prisoner to the City Police Court
Coleman, William	Cabdriver who drove the Prisoner from the York Minster to the Locomotive Inn
Coxon, Thomas	Friend of John Parkey
Doughty, William	Police Constable who saw Oldfield in Robinson's cab and accompanied him to the Royal Infirmary
Dreschfold, Julius	Professor of Pathology at Manchester's Victoria University
Eastwood, Thomas	Friend of the Prisoner who saw him get into a cab near the Cathedral steps on February 26th
Estcourt, Charles	Analyst to the City of Manchester
Estcourt, Phillip	Clerk and son of Charles Estcourt
Fletcher, John	The Victim
Fletcher, Robert	The Victim's nephew.
Frost, Mary	Landlady of the Three Arrows
Goodfellow, Thomas	Physician who attended to Oldfield at the Royal Infirmary
Goulding, Harry	Cabdriver who drove the Victim and the Prisoner to the Three Arrows and Stretford Road on February 26th
Gumpert, Edward	Local Manchester physician who wrote to the *British Medical Journal*
Hall, William	Business associate of the Victim who saw him at the Mitre Hotel.

Hampden-Parker, John	House physician at the Royal Infirmary
Headlam, Francis	The Stipendiary at the City Police Court
Heywood, Samuel	Indian-rubber manufacturer who knew the Victim and saw him leaving the Three Arrows with the Prisoner
Hocklin, Walter	The Victim's family solicitor at the Coroner's and City Police Courts
Holt, Andrew	Landlord of the York Minster
Hopwood, Charles	Recorder of Liverpool and counsel for the prosecution at the Prisoner's trial at the Liverpool Assizes
Jackson, Robert	Police Constable who communicated to the Chief Detective Inspector the reported poisoning of Parkey
Jakeman, William	Police Constable who saw Goulding's cab leave and return to the Monument cab stand on February 26th
Lait, Edward	Seller of dried fish and game at 10, Victoria Street, adjoining Sinclair's oyster rooms
Lushington, Godfrey	Secretary of State representative who responded to Burton's letter requesting a reprieve for the Prisoner
McKeand, Charles	Council for the defence at the Prisoner's trial at the Liverpool Assizes
Miller, John	Police Constable to whom Phillips gave his evidence at the Detective Office
Moxon, Alfred	Barman at the Crown and Anchor where the Prisoner, his brother, Parkey and Coxon went drinking together
Mutten, Jessie	Barman at the Blue Boar Hotel where the Prisoner and Oldfield went drinking together
Needham, John	Working man who saw the Prisoner alight from Goulding's cab in Stretford Road
Oldfield, Samuel	Grocer drugged and robbed by the Prisoner on January 8th, 1889
Parkey, John	Porter drugged and robbed by the Prisoner on December 28th, 1888

LIST OF CHARACTERS

Parton, Augustus	The Prisoner's brother
Parton, Charles	The Prisoner
Parton, "Pig Jack"	The Prisoner's father
Pearson, Emily	Housekeeper to her step-father, Andrew Holt, landlord of the York Minster
Phillips, Andrew	Bookkeeper who saw the Prisoner pore liquid from a vial into a glass of beer at the Three Arrows
Reynolds, Ernest	Resident medical officer at the Royal Infirmary
Robinson, Thomas	Cabdriver who picked up the Prisoner and Oldfield in Todd Street after they left the Blue Boar Hotel
Smelt, Sidney	The Deputy Coroner
Smith, Harry	Employee of the tailor's lock-up at 43, Stretford Road
Spedding, Frank	Patron of the Three Arrows who saw the Prisoner and Victim drinking there on the evening of February 26th
Watts, David	Warehouseman who John Needham told that he saw the Prisoner alight from the cab in Stretford Road
Wild, George	Business associate of the Victim who saw him at the Mitre Hotel
Wilson, Samuel	Inspector in the Detectives Division, Manchester police force, and deputy to the Detective Chief Inspector
Wittaker, John	Housemate of the Prisoner in Moore Street, who saw him put money under his mattress
Yates, Alan	Manager of the London Dress Company and employer of Andrew Phillips

INTRODUCTION

The Crime

John Fletcher was an owner of Messrs. Robert Fletcher and Son, paper manufacturers. At the time of the case, he had retired from active participation and left day to day operations of the business to his nephew, Robert Fletcher. They had an office in Cannon Street, Manchester and a mill in Stoneclough, Radcliffe, between Manchester and Bolton. John Fletcher, who lived in Southport, arrived in Manchester on Tuesday, February 26th, 1889. He met his nephew at their company offices in the city centre. John Fletcher left about 1:15pm with the intention of attending at 4:30pm the sale of a mill being held at the Mitre Hotel in the city centre, located adjacent to the Cathedral. He was wearing an expensive gold watch and carrying a considerable amount of cash in his purse. Fletcher was next seen at the Mitre Hotel around 5pm by business associates. Fletcher was somewhat of a drinker and although nobody knows what he did between 1:15 and 5pm, it is a safe bet that he was out boozing. He was described as being under the influence of drink by a witness at the Mitre Hotel.

Parton left the Mitre Hotel and walked to the Shambles.

Fletcher left the Mitre Hotel alone and planned on going to Sinclair's oyster rooms, in Victoria Street. He did not end up going there but was seen around 6:40pm by the proprietor of a dried fish stall in Victoria Street, first walking alone from the direction of the Shambles (an area of market stalls, butcher's shops and pubs off Victoria Street), and then in the company of a young man. The two companions talked together for a few minutes and then walked to the Cathedral and hailed a cab from the Monument (Cromwell's statue) cab stand. They were observed by Police Constable William Jakeman. They took the cab, driven by Harry Goulding, a short distance down Deansgate to the Three Arrows public house at the corner with St Mary's Street. They stayed for one drink and then took the same cab towards the address 43, Stretford Road. On route, the cabman's attention was drawn to the fact that one of his customers had done a runner. Goulding got down from the driver's seat of the cab and found that young man had disappeared and Fletcher was comatose in the cab. Not knowing what to do, he returned to the Monument stand where PC Jakeman was still on duty. Jakeman joined Goulding on the driver's seat and took Fletcher to the Royal Infirmary in Piccadilly. He died while being conveyed into the hospital. Inspection of the deceased body and clothing showed that his watch and cash were missing.

Chief Detective Inspector Caminada was brought in to investigate the day after the incident. Jerome Caminada was Manchester's most celebrated detective and in 1895 he published a book describing his experiences as a Manchester policeman, entitled, *Twenty-Five Years of Detective Life*. In 1901 he published a second volume of his memoirs. His most famous case was the "Manchester Cab Mystery."

Caminada had no idea who the young man was and only had rough descriptions. Using his renowned detective skills he rapidly traced the movements of the youth to the York Minster pub in Higher Chatham Street within a few minutes of him jumping from the cab, and then via a second cab to the Locomotive Inn on Oldham Road, a notorious haunt for members of the boxing fraternity. Through his knowledge of the unsavoury characters who frequented the Locomotive Inn, Caminada focused on Charles Parton as the likely culprit. Within about 72 hours of execution of the crime, Caminada had identified his prime suspect.

Charles Parton was from the Ancoats region of the city and was born on the wrong side of the tracks. Despite his age he was a chronic criminal – at the time of this arrest he was only twenty years old.

Early on Saturday morning, March 2nd, Parton was arrested and charged with robbery and on suspicion of having caused the death of John Fletcher. At noon the same day, "amid many manifestations of esteem and sympathy," the remains of John Fletcher were interred in the family vault attached to the ancient parish church of Radcliffe.

Once in custody Parton was identified by a number of witnesses who had seen him and Fletcher together on the evening in question, and he was then formally charged.

Meanwhile, post mortem analysis of the body revealed that Fletcher's death was due to syncope (a sudden loss of consciousness due to insufficient blood supply to the brain), and despite the fact that Fletcher had heart disease as a result of excessive alcohol intake, Fletcher's death was attributed to syncope without obvious cause. The problem was apparently solved when the city analyst detected the presence of chloral in the body fluids of the deceased.

Chloral is an organic compound that exists as a colourless oily liquid. It was first synthesised in 1832, simply through the chlorination of ethanol. It dissolves in water to form chloral hydrate, which was the first depressant developed for the specific purpose of inducing sleep. It is a sedative and hypnotic drug whose properties were first published in 1869 and subsequently, because of its easy synthesis, its use became widespread. It takes effect in a relatively short time (about 30 minutes) and will induce sleep in an hour. It was widely used recreationally and misprescribed in the late nineteenth century. It was often used by alcoholics whose sleep patterns had become disturbed by excessive drinking. Chloral is soluble in both water and alcohol, and readily forms concentrated solutions. In Victorian England, a solution of chloral and alcohol constituted the infamous "knockout drops" or "Mickey Finn." Much more recently, chloral hydrate has been used as a date rape drug.

In addition, by questioning Parton, Caminada was able to link Parton with the theft of chloral from a chemist's shop in Liverpool a week prior to the crime. Parton had entered the shop under the pretext of needing chloral for his mother who he claimed suffered from *angina pectoris*. He did not have the required prescription but persuaded the chemist to let him have a few grains. While the chemist was dispensing this, Parton stole the whole bottle containing one pound of chloral. Charles Hopwood, council for the prosecution at the trial of Parton in Liverpool commented that *angina pectoris* is not "terminology used by people of the prisoner's class of life." However, Dr Ernest Reynolds, Resident Medical Officer, Manchester Royal Infirmary, gave evidence that about six weeks prior to the case, he had a patient in one of the medical wards of the Infirmary suffering from an aneurism, with disease of the heart and *angina pectoris*. The patient, to whom he probably prescribed chloral, recently revealed himself to be Parton's father. Consequently, it was argued that this situation had enabled Parton to use such specific knowledge with the chemist.

Meanwhile, reports of the case in the newspapers prompted the uncovering of two very similar cases of drugging for the purpose of robbery committed by Parton in December 1888 and January 1889: John Parkey, a porter, and Samuel Oldfield, a grocer, curiously both from Ashton-under-Lyne. Perhaps those from the eastern suburbs were particularly gullible. In both cases, they met up with Parton in a city centre pub and at the end of the evening found themselves drugged and robbed. Parkey was a young man and became seriously ill as a result of the drugging. He lingered in agony for months, and died a few days after Parton's conviction, never having recovered from the effects of the drug administered.

Following Parton's arrest, there followed a whirl wind of court appearances, all within a week – eight in total; three at the Coroner's Court and five before the City Police Court. The Coroner's Court was assessing whether the death of Fletcher was accidental and the City Police Court was reviewing the evidence to remand the prisoner in custody and commit him to trial if supported by the evidence. However, there was much duplication of proceedings at the two courts which made for highly inefficient judicial proceedings. Indeed, Caminada himself considered the process of having to present both before the Coroner's and Magistrates Court, an inefficient use of resources, which he discussed in Volume II of his memoirs.

> The original Coroner's Act of Edward I, which gave an appointed official the right to inquire into the cause of sudden death within his jurisdiction, was no doubt at that comparatively lawless period an eminently necessary piece of legislation. Nor has the law ceased to be useful even in the present time. In remote districts the inevitable coroner's inquiry, which is sure to follow any and every case of sudden and violent death, is a precautionary measure for the safety of the lieges; it acts as a deterrent against crime, and assists criminal courts in arriving at just verdicts. But it is felt that in cities and large towns the coroner's court is but an expensive and withal fussy ante-chamber to the justice room of the stipendiary magistrates, and that some alteration is needed in the conduct of its inquiries. The double investigation which now takes place before the coroner and the magistrate, in cases where a person is accused of crime in relation to a sudden death, is a needless waste of public and private time, money, and convenience.

However, court proceedings were certainly efficient in some respects. For example, Parton was arrested at 12:30 am on Saturday and later the same morning, Parton's first appearance at the City Police Court took place. In only a few hours the court had been convened with three magistrates on the bench and five witnesses to testify that Parton was the young man seen in the company of Fletcher on the night in question. The witnesses had previously gone to the Town Hall to identify the prisoner in the police cells. This seems remarkable at a time when sophisticated methods of communication were not widely available. The result of the appearance was the remand of the prisoner until Monday by the Court.

For all appearances the courts were filled to over flowing with spectators. It appears that the population viewed such occasions as a cheap form of entertainment, particularly when cases of a "sensational" nature were being investigated.

Examination of the case at the Coroner's Court was before the Deputy Coroner, Sidney Smelt, not the Coroner himself. Caminada described the process of the Court issuing warrants commanding attendance before the Coroner in Volume II of his memoirs and discusses the irony of the absence of the Coroner himself.

> "By the virtue of a warrant," so the document began, which, authorised and issued under the hand and seal of Her Majesty's Coroner, and signed by the Chief Constable, required you to personally appear in a certain Court, on a given date, and there to inquire on Her Majesty's behalf into the death of the deceased paper maker. The reader may have received such a document before, and have responded to the request expressed in it, in which case, probably, he will feel like the Yankee who confessed that he had tasted "biled crow," but couldn't say that he hankered after it. This feeling will be intensified if it should happen that such a document

should be presented at an inconvenient season, for instance, when you have made preparations to go away for a holiday, in which case the prospect of having to view dead bodies when you had hoped to view landscapes will doubtless cause a feeling of dissatisfaction. If the consciousness of having had greatness and responsibility thrust upon you should have the effect of lifting you up in your own esteem, such self-satisfaction will be qualified when you read in the summons that you must not fail to appear at your peril, and that you are not to depart without leave. In one sense, then, you are both a judge and prisoner.

When the day comes the coroner opens the proceedings by reciting to you the authority by which he holds the inquiry, and informs you that he is there as the deputy of the gentleman whose name appears on the summons, and who, it seems, is unavoidably absent. From this you learn that a coroner's duties may be performed vicariously – a privilege which, doubtless, you will be inclined to regret is not extended to his jurymen.

During the initial proceedings in Manchester, Parton was not represented by defence council due to the "want of funds." Ten minutes prior to his second appearance at the City Police Court, William Burton was appointed to appear on his behalf. He also represented Parton at the Coroner's Court after his appointment. No information seems available on Burton's experience but he appeared singularly ineffective in defending the prisoner. He was certainly no match for William Cobbett, retained by the police to present the evidence to the City Police Court in an effort to have Parton committed to trial. Consequently, based on the evidence presented, the Coroner's Court found Parton guilty of wilful murder and the City Police Court committed Parton to trial at the Liverpool Assizes on all charges preferred against him: drugging John Parkey and Samuel Oldfield in order to steal their property; robbing and slaying John Fletcher; and stealing one pound of chloral from a chemist's shop in Liverpool. No closing statement was made by Burton at either the City Police Court or at the Coroner's Court: Burton simply stated that the prisoner had a complete answer to all the charges against him and at the proper time it would be presented. It never was.

It is curious to note that the jury at the Coroner's Court, after finding the prisoner guilty of "willful murder," offered their compliments to Caminada on the skills displayed by him in the execution of his duties, and recommended him for a reward.

Parton appeared at the Liverpool Assizes on March 18th and 19th before Justice Charles. Council for the prosecution was Charles Hopwood, Q.C., Recorder of Liverpool, an experienced lawyer described as the "learned Recorder of Liverpool" by the Judge. The prisoner was defended by Charles McKeand. The Court proceeded to try Parton only for the slaying of John Fletcher and for the theft of chloral. Parton pleaded not guilty. He was certainly better defended at Liverpool than he was at the earlier proceedings in Manchester.

The prosecution thought the fact that Fletcher was a heavy drinker and that his health was suffering from the chronic effects of alcohol was a weakness in their case. On a number of occasions Fletcher was referred to as being "in his usual health" by prosecuting councel to deflect the thinking that Fletcher may have been responsible for his own death and actually died of alcohol poisoning. Hopwood specifically referred to this in his opening statement.

> Now, an aspersion has been cast upon the character of the deceased that he indulged far too freely in liquors. It is a question as to how this circumstance, if true, coincided with the appearance of the deceased, and as to how far that might have had its effect in connection with the administration of a drug. The medical men believe that there was nothing in the disease of the heart that caused his death. It might be that that disease might go on, and it might be a question of days or months, but there was nothing to account for death. It is possible, in the ingenuity of the learned gentlemen who defend the prisoner, that it might be suggested that a man who was diseased about the heart was more likely to succumb to the influence of a deadly drug than a man who was perfectly healthy. That matters not to me representing justice, nor to you as inquirers in the interest of justice. If the prisoner by his acts accelerated Mr Fletcher's death by a single day he is guilty of murder. It matters not what other causes might combine to cause death, and it matters not whether the unfortunate man was, to some extent, the worse for drink before the drug was administered. He was in his usual state of health, and whether the fact that he was in drink, or whether the fact that he was to some extent diseased internally, formed a fertile ground upon which poison may take effect was immaterial, if his death was accelerated by that poison it is murder.

The judicial proceedings hinged on the forensic evidence. The case was complicated since the drug chloral was little understood at the time. The prosecution argued that the evidence pointed to murder. The defence suggested that Fletcher was responsible for his own death. The expected, initial approach of the defence, to challenge the identification of Parton being the young man responsible, was thwarted before the case began by the multitude of witnesses who had identified Parton. The result of the *post-mortem* was that Fletcher had died of syncope, due to failure of the heart's action, which was not due to disease. The death was attributed to a combination of chloral and alcohol.

However, since there was no direct evidence, only circumstantial evidence, that Parton had drugged Fletcher with chloral, the next approach of the defence was to argue that Fletcher was responsible for his own death. They used two arguments. First, that Fletcher had not died from chloral poisoning at all by challenging the quality of the analytical chemistry and arguing that chloral was not present. They argued that syncope was due to alcohol alone on a body diseased by long, continued abuse of alcohol – Fletcher had a gin drinker's liver, partial fatty degeneration of the heart, partial congestion of the lungs and all his organs more or less affected by drink. Consequently, Fletcher had died of simple alcohol poisoning. Secondly, if chloral were present, and death was a result of alcohol and chloral combined, the chloral might have been self-administered, if Fletcher routinely used chloral, for example, to help him sleep – a common usage at the time particularly for heavy drinkers. This second argument seems the one that should have been pursued vigorously, but was not explored in detail by the defence, only mentioned during cross examination.

The final position of the defence was that the medical evidence had left the cause of death so much in doubt that the prisoner should be given the benefit of that doubt. Indeed, Dr John Hampden-Barker, the receiving physician at the Royal Infirmary initially diagnosed simple alcohol poisoning. Chloral was identified in Fletcher's body fluids as a result of the suggestion from Chief Detective Inspector Caminada once he traced the culprit to the pugilistic community where it was used in "knockout drops" in boxing circles. Indeed, none of the medical witnesses would pledge their professional reputation that Fletcher did not die from alcohol poisoning alone. Hampden-Barker reported that there was slight fatty degeneration of the heart and a man in such a condition was more likely to be affected by drink than a man who was healthy. Had he not known that chloral had been detected, Hampden-Barker would have expressed the opinion that Fletcher had died of alcohol poisoning.

However, Parton's defence took a couple of powerful hooks and then a knockout punch during the judicial proceedings. The two hooks, although still circumstantial, were late in the proceedings in Manchester, when Parton was linked with the theft of chloral from a chemist in Liverpool and to the earlier poisoning of two other individuals under very similar circumstances. The knock-out punch to the defence came at the trial in Liverpool with the almost sensational appearance of a witness who had not given evidence at the earlier judicial proceedings in Manchester. Andrew Phillips testified that he saw Parton pour some fluid from a small vial into a glass of beer in the Three Arrows on the night in question. This testimony of direct evidence sealed the fate of Parton – he is now known to be in possession of chloral and observed pouring an unknown liquid into a glass of beer. There is no suggestion that Phillips was anything other than a genuine witness, but his appearance was very convenient for the prosecution.

McKeand during the trial was not particularly effective in cross-examining witnesses but did make some interesting statements with respect to the case in his closing remarks. First, he commented that it was totally unfair that he was only given notice on Friday night, the trial starting on the Monday, that a new witness, Phillips, was to appear. He did not have time to inquire into Phillips' reputation and to investigate his evidence such as how long he had been at the Three Arrows. Secondly, McKeand challenged Phillip's motivation and considered unbelievable his excuse for not coming forward earlier, that he did not want to lose his job and did not consider his evidence material. He implied his appearance was motivated by his moment of glory. Thirdly, playing on the argument that Fletcher was responsible for his own death, McKeand argued that just because Parton robbed Fletcher it did not follow that Parton drugged and killed him. "Assuming for the purpose of argument that the prisoner did not administer chloral, what was more natural, if he were a thief, as the prosecution suggested he was, than that he, seeing Mr Fletcher in the cab in a condition more or less comatosed from drink, should seize the opportunity of relieving him of his watch and guard and getting away?" Fourthly, he challenged the quality of the forensic data although he did recognize that his knowledge of the subject was limited. "I have done all I could with my limited knowledge to bring forward all the facts," and asked "in a question of life and death, whether it would be right to rely too implicitly upon it?" Fifthly, one of the strongest pieces of circumstantial evidence was 43, Stretford Road. When Fletcher and Parton left the Three Arrows, Parton instructed the cabbie to drive to that address. The prosecution argued that this was a "blind" – one chosen at random to give Parton time to act. In his closing statement McKeand challenged this for the first time. He implied that the location was a brothel, "a corner house in a neighbourhood of certain houses," but this was stated in such a typical, Victorian, low-key manner, that its impact on the jury was probably totally lost. Lastly, McKeand referred to the confusion around the case with respect to the medical evidence in a particularly striking phrase. "This case has been called the mystery of a four-wheeled cab, and it had been rightly called, because from first to last it has been enveloped in perfect clouds of mystery and doubt, which you have today been asked to unravel."

However, such arguments were too few and too late and Parton was found guilty by the jury within twenty minutes, but they did recommend him to mercy on account of his age.

It is interesting to note that the detailed publication of the judicial proceedings against Parton at Manchester in the newspapers, brought forward much of the evidence against Parton, including the identification of Philips and the uncovering of the two additional cases of poisoning. Hopwood referred to this is his opening statement at the trial, stating that the jury might have already heard facts around the case.

> It has been the subject of comment, and the facts might have reached the ears of some of you, but in all these matters it is necessary to remember that

> if publicity was no disadvantage to the prisoner it was an advantage to the prosecution. Several instances will occur in the course of the trial which will demonstrate that publicity has been useful to the ends of justice. However, I caution you against yielding to any preconceived notions with regard to the facts of the case. You are gentlemen assembled under the sanction of the law to try a fellow citizen upon a grave charge and I am sufficiently persuaded of your general fairness of conduct to trust you to the task.

It seems reasonable to assume that the jury were fully familiar with the case and had already read about the evidence in the newspapers. This seems far from a fair trial that we expect today and the situation was clearly not "no disadvantage to the prisoner."

The evidence of the presence of chloral in Fletcher's body fluids is somewhat unconvincing. The analyst himself, Charles Estcourt, admitted that the test is an "exceedingly delicate" one at the Coroner's Court, although he denied using the word "exceedingly" at the Liverpool trial. At the trial he also admitted that this was the first time an analysis of chloral had been made for a Court of Justice and that this was the first case he had been called upon to perform such an analysis. The data was not challenged aggressively by the defence and the evidence from the "medical men" appeared to be treated as gospel, and only challenged in the politest ways by the defence. We know better today the fallibility of so called "expert witnesses." Chloral was only introduced into the case when the culprit was linked to boxing where it was used as "knock-out drops." Chloral seems to have pervaded the whole case from this point onwards, and the analyst challenged to detect it.

Although the chloral analysis was unconvincing, the mode of death and other *post-mortem* observations did strongly point to chloral poisoning. For example, *post-mortem* clots are generally found in some part of the body. Parton's blood was found to be fluid throughout the body. This is a very characteristic side effect of chloral poisoning. Congestion of the lungs and slight congestion of the membranes of the brain also point to chloral poisoning. The mode of death was also consistent with chloral and not alcohol poisoning as pointed out by Dr Julius Dreschfold, Professor of Pathology at Victoria University, and expert witness for the prosecution.

> A person having had a large dose of ardent spirits, such as a half pint or pint of whisky, might die suddenly. Death might also be caused by fatty degeneration of the heart or extensive hemorrhage of the brain. In the deceased I found incipient fatty degeneration of the heart and slight congestion of the brain, but no hemorrhage of the brain. If for an hour before death Mr Fletcher was drinking beer and sherry, that certainly excludes the notion that he died from an overdose of spirits. Seeing that the deceased had been walking about an hour before death there was certainly no coma. The fact that death occurred so soon after was incompatible with

the theory of death by alcoholic poisoning, inasmuch as there was only partial insensibility not many minutes before death. It was a case of death by sudden syncope. There was also the circumstance that the deceased was described as having walked from the Three Arrows less than an hour before. That would not indicate alcoholic coma. The condition in which I found the body of the deceased was consistent with death by chloral.

There is absolutely no doubt that Parton administered chloral to Fletcher. The evidence against him is simply overwhelming. First, he was known to be in possession of chloral which he stole from a chemist shop in Liverpool. He was identified by the pharmacist Charles Bromley. Secondly, he was known to have executed two similar crimes previously. The two victims, Parkey and Oldfield, both survived, and identified Parton as the culprit. Thirdly, Parton was identified by a multitude of witnesses as the young man who was with Fletcher on the night in question. Fourthly, Andrew Phillips saw Fletcher pour the contents of a small round bottle into a glass of beer in the Three Arrows. Finally, Parton grew up in a family that knew the properties of chloral. His father, "Pig Jack," drugged the patrons of his public house by adding chloral to their beer so that he could rob them. He also arranged and bet on boxing contests and found it profitable to drug the mouth wash provided to the opponents of his fighters.

However, what is equally certain was that Parton had no intention of killing Fletcher. As he had done twice previously, his intention was to "hocuse" (stupefy with drugged liquor) Fletcher in order to relieve him of his watch and money. Consequently, Parton was really guilty of manslaughter. However, at the time the law was clear: if one person administered a stupefying drug to another with the intention of robbing him, and death ensued on administration of the drug, then the person who administered it is guilty of willful murder. Consequently, Parton was found guilty and sentenced to death.

The report of the police investigation showed Caminada to be a methodical, determined and creative detective in the way he hunted down the culprit. Caminada did display a certain degree of arrogance exemplified by statements in his memoirs covering the case, such as, "I now began to consider the case seriously, for it became evident that if the young man was to be arrested I should have to rely on my own judgment" after he traced the culprit to the Locomotive Inn. His memoirs of the case also included a vivid and colourful description of the "free and easy" entertainment taking place in a pub in Market Place. This was typical of the entertainment that took place in many of the pubs at the time, and the performers and performances were of a particularly poor quality. "But here comes the sweet songstress, and we soon find that she has only about three notes, two at the top and one at the bottom of the scale, which we hear alternately amidst the uproarious applause of her fascinated mashers below."

Whilst watching such entertainment in the Slip Inn, Oldfield meets Parton and the two start drinking together.

Following the trial, commentaries on the case were published in the major newspapers. Such reports contained some very colourful language. For example, the *Manchester Courier* described Parton in the following way. "The miserable culprit was a prominent figure amongst 'fast' young men. He had acquired some skill as a boxer; and the loose habits that skill induced, and the disreputable company into which it brought him, blunted his moral nature and made him a thief." The London *Daily Telegraph* described the efficiency with which Parton was brought to justice as "laudable promptitude" and described a crime that "presented more than one feature of peculiar vileness." The *Liverpool Courier* described Parton's behaviour as "precociousness in fiendish arts."

Some reports also discussed the case in terms of contemporary issues. For example, the London *Daily Telegraph* praised the success of the Manchester police in bringing the culprit to book just a few months after "Jack the Ripper" had evaded discovery. "The knowledge that atrocious criminals – such as the perpetrator of the Whitechapel butcheries, for instance – have succeeded in evading discovery for many months and are still at liberty (in all probability rubbing shoulders daily with well-conducted and law-abiding persons), is heavily fraught with mortification to the people of a civilised country." The *Manchester Guardian* discussed the case within the context of the famous Palmer and Dove strychnine poisoning cases thirty years earlier when the qualities of that drug were not well understood. The article concluded that the detection of chloral by the men of science served the cause of public safety since "persons who might be disposed to imitate Parton's method should know that this latest form of secret poisoning is just as liable to detection as were the commoner forms of murder by the administration of strychnine or other deadly ingredients."

The case also created a medical debate that unfolded in the *British Medical Journal* Dr Gumpert, a local physician of Manchester wrote a letter to the journal essentially disagreeing with the outcome of the trial. He criticized the lack of experts and the absence of a council of specially appointed forensic medical men to approve forensic testing. He pointed out that only three weeks had elapsed between the crime and the sentencing, the time it would take – at least on the Continent – to make a thorough chemical analysis, and write a medical report on the symptoms exhibited by the deceased, on the *post-mortem* examination, and on the result of the chemical analysis. He also argued that cases of, for example, adulterated milk, were taken more seriously and many people were under the impression that property is held much more sacred than human life. Gumpert asserted that a perpetration of injustice had taken place. He argued that the chemical analysis recording only traces of chloral was incompatible with the assumption that a quantity of chloral had been administered to Fletcher large enough to have caused his death and that death was due to syncope as a result of alcohol acting on a fatty heart. Both Dr Julius Dreschfold and Dr Ernest Reynolds replied separately to Gumpert's letter and disputed his assertion but this tended toward essentially a rehash of the confusing medical evidence presented at the trial. Nevertheless, Dreschfold pointed out the danger in such an argument since "the same plea might be set up in all cases of criminal deaths where the victim had taken some spirituous liquor shortly before death, and where the necropsy revealed fatty degeneration of the heart and liver – a combination of factors which surely is often found to exist." However, the definitive argument to refute Gumpert came when Reynolds published his "Medical Opinion" of the case in the same journal a number of months later. Reynolds argued that the when a poison is found in a very small quantity it is inevitably argued that it was insufficient to cause death; but the quantity found in the stomach is only the surplus of the amount already absorbed and sufficient to cause death.

In the 1920s, Parton published his own account of the tragedy. In this account he does admit to robbing Fletcher, but not to murdering him. "When I jumped from the cab Fletcher was alive and unhurt. I used no violence whatever and had no doubt that the man would be fine and well by the following day. Little could I have known that, a few moments later, he would be dead."

He certainly played down his role in the poisoning. His story was that one day he was walking along Deansgate when he met some "racing gang" associates in the company of John Fletcher, who they knew was carrying a lot of money. Parton joined them and they went to a public house, where one of the gang placed some chloral hydrate in Fletcher's drink. Fletcher rapidly began to get restless and Parton left with him giving his associates the wink that he would finish the job. Clearly, this account is not consistent with the evidence. Fletcher was only seen in the company of Parton, and Parton was the one observed adding poison to the beer.

However, Parton's account does give some very interesting insights into life in prison in the late nineteenth and early twentieth centuries. Parton was sentenced to be executed on April 9th but was reprieved on April 6th based on the recommendation to mercy by the jury that was supported by the Judge. Parton spent several weeks in Kirkdale Prison, initially in the condemned cell and then in the ordinary cells following his reprieve. Before his reprieve came through, Parton describes the conditions under which he had to say good-bye to his family.

> I broke down only once in the condemned cell. My mother and father, brothers and sister, came to say good bye. The parting took place in a room divided into two by iron bars. I was on one side of the room, my loved ones on the other. In the middle and between us was a passage-way with iron bars on both sides, and up and down this a warder walked to make

sure we did not try to shake hands. Two other warders were there to make sure no signs were passed.

I was not even allowed a farewell kiss from my mother. All I could do was to stand in my blue prison clothes and read the misery of my dear ones. When the interview, which lasted only a few minutes, was over and I was led away, my tiny sister called out, "This way, Charlie," and pointed to the door they had come in by. She thought I was at liberty to go with them, not knowing my life was forfeit.

From Kirkdale, Parton was transferred to Stafford Jail and then to Portland. It was three years before he "was granted the privilege and luxury of a cup of tea." At Stafford he was kept in solitary confinement, was only allowed out of his cell for one hour in twenty-four and was kept at work making slippers. At Portland, convicts, insufficiently fed, were required to work in the quarries and given "superhuman" tasks to accomplish. Self mutilation was common to avoid the work. The cell in which he lived for nine years was seven feet high, six feet long and three feet wide – a man over six feet was unable to lie down.

Following Portland, Parton spent two years in Dartmoor from which he was released. Parton believed that medical evidence eventually demonstrated that Fletcher had died of heart failure and not poisoning, and that he should be pardoned and released. This is clearly a very partisan interpretation of the medical debate. However, he was never pardoned for the crime but was released on a "ticket-of-leave," a revocable permit issued to a convicted person whose sentence has not expired, giving them conditional liberty. Parton considered this license to be totally unreasonable.

> It is laid down that I must not "lead an idle and dissolute life, without visible means of obtaining an honest livelihood." Once every month I must report to the police, and if I stir beyond the district in which I reside I must give the authorities a reason for my movements. I am prohibited from being found in or upon any dwelling-house, or any building, yard or premises being parcel of or attached to such dwelling house, or in or upon any shop, warehouse, counting-house, or other place of business, or in any garden or orchard, pleasure ground, and so on, without being able to account to the satisfaction of the court for my being there. Imagine it! If I am found sitting in a public park and I am unable to prove that quiet enjoyment is my sole reason for being there, I can be sent to prison again, to remain there until death gives me release.

In contravention of his "ticket-of leave," Parton visited Canada, South Africa and New Zealand before settling in Argentina where he established a café business.

He only returned to England to enlist in the First World War but immediately fell in trouble with the police. He ended up spending an additional ten years in prison after his release on a "ticket-of-leave" and "all for trivial offences." Eventually, Parton made a living "going round the country selling copies of the very licence which brought all this misery upon me."

The Chief Detective Inspector

Caminada was Chief Detective Inspector in the Manchester police force at the time of the "Cab Mystery." He was born in Deansgate, Manchester in 1844, to an Irish mother and an Italian father. At that time Deansgate consisted mostly of public houses, brothels, and poor quality housing for mill workers, and was the heart of Victorian Manchester's crime world.

In the early 1800s, Italy was not a country, but a number of small warring states and poverty was rife. Migration to Northern Europe was common at the time. Francis Caminada of Lombardy was among such immigrants. He arrived in England via Ireland. By 1843, he was married to Mary Boyle, from Ireland, living at 33, Peter Street in Manchester, opposite the Free Trade Hall, and made his living as a cabinet maker. Francis' brother, Louis, also lived in Manchester, and was recorded in 1822 as a shopkeeper in Lees Street, off Great Ancoats Street.

Although it is not documented how many children were born to Francis and Mary Boyle, they did register a son in the name of Ambrose on March 30th, 1844. The child was born on March 5th, 1844, but it appears that between the registration date and the baptism, the child's name was changed to that of Jerome. Jerome Caminada was educated at St Mary's Catholic School on Mulberry Street, just off Brazennose Street, directly opposite the Town Hall. The family worshipped at St Mary's church, colloquially known as the "Hidden Gem," also located on Mulberry Street, and still an active place of worship. He remained throughout his life a staunch Roman Catholic, a teetotaler and a family man.

Caminada was fortunate to receive a good education, and unlike the vast majority of the population, was literate when he left school. Upon leaving he began working as an engineer at the ironworks of Messrs. Sharp and Stewart and afterwards at the works of Messrs. Mather & Platts. He was also a member of the police reserve. In February 1868, at age twenty-four, Caminada joined the Manchester City Police as an ordinary constable and was attached to the A Division under Superintendent Gee.

He spent most of his early life as a single man, living in lodgings. In 1881 he was living at 4, Oxford Grove, Chorlton-on-Medlock. He lodged with Peter Marno, a twenty-eight-year-old Scottish born Police Constable, and his wife. In the same year, aged thirty-seven, he married Amelia Wainhouse at the nearby church of the Holy Name on Oxford Road. Caminada thereafter lived for some years with his wife and mother-in-law, Mary Wainhouse, at 22, Eastnor Street, Stretford. The family later moved to Denmark Road in Moss Side.

Even though infant mortality was rife at the time, the Caminadas appeared to suffer more than most. Between 1883 and 1886, Amelia gave birth to three children, Louis, Mary Amelia and Charles, all of whom died in infancy. However, on December 10th, 1887 another male child was born and given the name Charles Bernard. This son survived and was recorded as being present at the death of Caminada.

Caminada was a policeman from 1868 until 1899. At that time, Manchester had a police force of around 800 strong, and the city was a hotbed of poverty, illness, deprivation and crime. While serving as a constable he showed much aptitude for detective work. This was recognized and in 1871 he was promoted to sergeant, and transferred to the newly formed Detectives Division. He remained a detective for the rest of his service. He rapidly made a name for himself, establishing national fame as the region's leading criminal detective.

In 1877, the town hall in Albert Square was opened with a police charge office and cells housed in the basement. Admittance was gained from the Lloyd Street entrance. This is where Caminada also had his office. From there he sallied forth day and night in plain clothes into the streets of Manchester. He knew all the back-alleys of the city and most of the villains who lived in them. Caminada was local and was often known as Detective Jerome to the area's criminals, who struggled to pronounce his last name.

In 1882, Caminada's reputation for policing earned him promotion to Inspector. In 1888 he was made Chief Inspector. His policing style was eccentric by modern standards; in those days, detectives were expected to use all kinds of disguises to penetrate communities that mistrusted the police in order to gather evidence on suspects. Caminada was reportedly a very talented "quick change" artist, fooling even those who knew him well. He also maintained a large network of informers, who he would often meet in the "Hidden Gem." His methods appeared to be effective since in 1897 he was appointed full Superintendent of the Detectives Division, the city's first Detective Superintendent. He is considered to be one of the greatest detectives ever to serve in the Manchester area.

Throughout his career, Caminada was reportedly responsible for the imprisonment of 1225 criminals and for the closure of 400 public houses because of the poor quality of the drinks or the lewd behaviour which was common in such places. He virtually cleaned up the streets of Manchester and as the city's prime thief taker, threats on his life were commonplace. Knowing he was a marked man, Caminada often used to carry a pistol, and had cause to use it on more than one occasion.

During the trying period of the dynamite conspiracy (a terrorist campaign which ran from 1880 to 1887 by Irish nationalists in support of their demands for independence from Britain), he was engaged in making inquiries in Ireland, France, Germany, and America. Also, he arrested a man named John Roberts at Leeds for what was known as the "Old Kent Road" murder, and for this he received the congratulations and thanks of Sir Edmund Henderson, the then Commissioner of the Metropolitan Police. But he was best known in Manchester, and as early as 1869 the Manchester Watch Committee rewarded him for the "creditable, discreet, and very satisfactory" discharge of certain important and confidential duties. In 1885 the Committee granted him £50 as a reward for valuable services rendered by him as chief of his department. In 1896 an address was presented to him by the Postmaster General, through the Watch Committee, for assistance in the detection and conviction of several men for telegraph frauds. On another occasion he received handsome rewards from two banks for the arrest of bank forgers. In June 1889, the Watch Committee unanimously carried a resolution to advance Chief Inspector Caminada's salary from £200 to £250 a year. A similar resolution in 1891 increased it from £250 to £276 per annum.

Caminada's thirty-year career brought him into contact with every conceivable type of criminal, from juvenile pickpockets to the army officer who tried to sell secrets to a foreign power. His cases varied from exposing quack doctors by posing as a patient, or hiding in a piano to catch a thief in the Free Trade Hall, to this famous hansom cab murder. Some of the most deeply laid schemes that he discovered were those of fraudulent advertisers, next-of-kin pretenders, lottery promoters, and registry office swindlers. In the conduct of prosecutions, his intelligence, the thoroughness with which he prepared his case, and his knowledge of criminal law, earned him the respect of colleagues, criminals, magistrates and the Assize Judges, by whom he was often complimented in court.

Caminada retired as a Detective Superintendent at the then age limit of fifty-five in 1899. He was awarded an unprecedented pension of £210 per annum and also received a special resolution in appreciation of his long, energetic and zealous service. Caminada lived for a further fifteen years after his retirement. He worked in self-employment and devoted himself to the business of an Estate and Enquiry Agent and to the management of property, chiefly in Rusholme and Moss Side. For three years he was actively engaged in municipal work. In 1907 he became the representative on the Manchester City Council of the Openshaw Ward, standing as an Independent candidate. In 1910 he stood again for Openshaw. The voting resulted in a tie, with Caminada and his opponent, Mr G. F. Titt, of the Labour party, each receiving 1482 votes. The Presiding Officer, Mr Alderman Hassall, gave his casting vote in favour of Titt, who was therefore elected. Caminada did not stand again.

Caminada died at his home in Mount St Bernard, 2 Denmark Road, Moss Side on March 10th, 1914, just five days prior to his seventieth birthday. He suffered from diabetes in the last six years of his life. His funeral took place at Manchester's Southern Cemetery where he was buried. Requiem mass was celebrated at the Church of the Holy Name. The Lord Mayor of Manchester, Alderman McCabe, was present, together with several magistrates from the City Police Court, including Mr R. A. Armitage. Deputations were present representing the Catholic Federation, the Men's Sodality, Holy Name, the Property Owners' Association, and the Ratepayers' Association. Of the many tributes he received, it is said that the one he would have valued most came from Judge Parry, who said: "A man of resource, energy and initiative, and never stultified by a petty adherence to regulations. He was the Garibaldi of detectives." Jerome Caminada was very proud of his father and his Italian ancestry and would have been delighted with his comparison to the great Italian patriot. He left a widow and a son and daughter. It was reported that, "He left an estate of the gross value of £16,527."

Caminada died, in part, as a result of injuries he had received in a bus accident in North Wales three years previously. In September 1911, he was on holiday at Rhyl, and on a Sunday afternoon he paid 3s. for a drive in a four horse coach to Llanfair and back. The coach had accommodation for 22 passengers, two sitting beside the driver and five on each of four long seats. On the return journey while the coach was coming down a very steep hill, Pont-y-Gwdell Hill near Pontygwyddr church where there is a sharp turn and where the road is very narrow, the horses shied at a heap of slates on the side of the road. The sudden swerve caused the coach to topple over. Nearly all the occupants were badly shaken, and three were seriously injured, although the coach and horses were unharmed, and the driver, the guard, and three of the passengers escaped without even a bruise. Mr Taylor of Chester and Caminada were so badly injured that they were removed to the Black Hotel, Llanfairtalhaiarn, where they were confined to bed. Miss Moore, of Rhyl, who had her back badly injured was taken home in a conveyance and remained under medical treatment. Taylor and Caminada received injuries to the legs, head and collar bone. Caminada was rendered unconscious by the accident and also had his nose and some ribs broken. He passed a very bad night and his relatives were summoned, and had to remain in bed nine days before he could be moved to Manchester, where he was bedridden for a further three weeks.

On March 12th, 1912, Caminada brought an action dealing with the liability of the coach proprietors for the safety of their passengers, before Mr Justice Bray and a special jury at the Manchester Assizes. Caminada, the plaintiff, was represented by Mr Tobin K. C., and the defendants, Messrs. Brookes Brothers, coach proprietors of Rhyl, were represented by Mr Langdon K. C. The action was to recover damages for injuries caused through alleged negligence on the part of the defendants. The case for the plaintiff was that the hill was a dangerous one, and that failure to ask some of the passengers to walk down it constituted neglect. In addition it was said that one of the brakes was not in good working order; that the driver was not physically strong enough to have charge of a coach with four horses; and that one of the leading horses was addicted to shying. The defence was that at the bottom of the hill one of the leading horses shied at a heap of slates, and that the driver was in no sense to blame. The jury found for the defendants and Caminada received no compensation.

Caminada's memoirs, published in 1895 and 1901, received great acclaim amidst competition at that time from the fictional character of Sherlock Holmes. Through these books he reminisced and told the story of detective life in a large northern slum city of Victorian England. The *Manchester Guardian* commented on his memoirs in an article reporting his death.

> A glance at its contents shows the extraordinary number and variety of his experiences. Only the most absolute self-reliance, with singular energy and unbound courage, could have carried him through contests of the severest kind with some of the most daring criminals. Not physical courage alone was demanded in the execution of his duties. He had to detect and expose some of the most crafty and experienced of criminals. How ingenious, persevering, and adroit such men often are is amply illustrated in his book. Mr. Caminada's undesirable acquaintances included every imaginable variety of offenders – cardsharpers, swindlers, burglars, forgers, coiners, reverend quacks, and ticket-of-leave men; and he was a familiar visitor to thieves' dens, gambling halls, and haunts of professional beggars.

The Prisoner

At the time of the case, Charles Parton had, for one so young, an eventful history. He was older by one year than he told the police when arrested. His birthplace was the city of Liverpool, where he was also condemned, and where his parents lived when he was born, in the year 1869. While he was a lad the family moved to Manchester, and Charles, after receiving a slender education became a messenger at a hotel in the city. Mr John Fletcher was one of the frequenters of this establishment, and it seems probable that the two new each other, at least by sight. Parton did not keep his situation long, and seemed to follow no regular employment afterwards. His father was at this time keeping a beerhouse in Greengate, Salford. The elder Parton was of considerable repute in the boxing world. He was known by the name of "Pig Jack," and described as the "9 st. 4 lb. champion of England." His family numbered three sons and a daughter. The boys copied the example of their father. Charles early acquired considerable skill as a boxer and led a "harum-scarum" life.

In 1887 he hurriedly left England for America under circumstances which reflected little credit on his honesty. His destination was Boston, and in that city he fraternized with boxing men. He made several appearances in public, advertised as the son of an English champion. The reason for his departure from the States is unknown, but he did not remain there for more than a few months. On his return to England he continued to lead a loose life. In company with a man older than himself, he traveled to Market Harborough, in Leicestershire, took lodgings in a hotel, and during the night, with the assistance of his confederate, rifled the place, and decamped with a quantity of jewellery. A few days afterwards he was found attempting to dispose of the stolen property in Northampton, and was arrested. For his offence he was committed to gaol for six weeks. He was in the clutches of the law again not very long after, being fined 21s. and costs, with the alternative of a term of imprisonment, at Stockport, for defrauding a railway company. On one other occasion the police had him in custody on a charge which was not sustained.

Following his return from America, Parton seemed to neglect his pugilistic exercises, but in the early part of 1889, he was trained for a performance at the Free Trade Hall, Manchester, arranged for the benefit of Jem Mace, England's first world heavyweight champion and the last of the great bare-fist fighters. He competed amongst the light weights, and won a second prize.

The period during which he had been guilty of the practice of using drugs to render his victims insensible before robbing them seems to have been confined to the last few months before his arrest for the murder of John Fletcher.

Although Parton pleaded not guilty to this crime at his trial in Liverpool, it was reported that he had previously acknowledged that he drugged Mr Fletcher. Whilst he was in custody at the Manchester Town Hall, a Manchester gentleman, who had known Parton's father, called and had an interview with him in one of the cells. They had some conversation about the case, and the report of this conversation is to the effect that the prisoner said he knew Mr Fletcher through the latter going to the hotel where Parton was engaged as messenger, that he met Mr Fletcher on the day of the murder, had some conversation with him, and then accompanied him to the Three Arrows Hotel, where he drugged him. "I gave him," Parton is reported to have said, "more than I intended, and when we came out of the Three Arrows, I saw he was a 'gonner,' so I put him in the cab, and got away as soon as I could." The police were not made aware of this conversation until after the trial. The gentleman to whom the statement is said to have been made was very reluctant to appear in the case, and at the time of the trial was unavoidably absent.

At the time of Charles' arrest, the Parton's resided in a *cul-de-sac* named Moore Street, off Rochdale Road. It was described as a very unpretentious street, and the few houses of which it was composed were small and dirty looking. The Manchester Weekly Times of March 23rd published the following article a few days after Parton had been sentenced to death.

> A visitor on the afternoon of the 22nd of March, found a very distressing state of affairs. A boy of about twelve summers, with a besmeared face (evidently through crying), answered the door, and beckoning the visitor to step into a parlour, he toddled upstairs for his mother. Mrs Parton soon made her appearance, and her swollen eyes testified to the pain she was suffering in consequence of the terrible doom before her son. Even the little child

she carried in her arms appeared uneasy because of its mother's trouble, and the faces of three other children who entered the room bore an aspect painful to behold. The group was shabbily dressed, and the room itself was but scantily furnished. The walls were hung with several lithographs illustrating renowned combats in the boxing ring, in which most of the male members of the Parton family have taken considerable interest. A number of photographs were also noticeable around the room, and among them were two of the son Charles, one representing the youth stripped to the waist, ready for a boxing encounter. Mrs Parton was scarcely able to speak owing to her trouble, and she broke into tears frequently when addressing her visitor. Among other matters she referred to the alleged confession by her son, and asserted that there was not a word of truth in the story.

On March 19th, Parton was sentenced to death at Liverpool Assizes. The High Sheriff of Lancashire later fixed Tuesday April 9th for the execution, "should the law take its course." He was conveyed to Kirkdale Prison and placed in the condemned cell.

Immediately on the sentence becoming known, steps were taken by the prisoner's solicitor, Mr William Burton, to give effect to the recommendation of mercy by the jury. A petition for presentation to the Home Secretary, "praying for a commutation of the death sentence," was prepared. Signatures were sought in Manchester and in Liverpool, where Parton was born. As a result, over one thousand signatures were obtained to the petition which was sent by train to London on Thursday, March 21st, for presentation to the Home Secretary.

On Saturday April 6th, Burton received the following letter.

> Sir – I am directed by the Secretary of State to inform you, with reference to the petition submitted by you in favour of Charles Parton who was sentenced to death for murder, that having regard to the recommendation of the prisoner to mercy by the jury, in which the learned judge concurred, the Secretary of State has felt himself justified in advising Her Majesty to respite the capital sentence, with a view to its commutation to penal servitude for life. – I am, sir, your obedient servant, Godfrey Lushington.

On February 3rd, 1904, the *Manchester Guardian* published an article entitled, "An Old Manchester Cab Mystery". It reported that Charles Parton, who in 1889 was sentenced to death for a murder in Manchester that attracted a great deal of attention at the time, but who was reprieved, had been released from prison. On December 28th, 1928, the same newspaper published an article entitled, "Man Once Sentenced To Death Returns To Goal."

Reference to a murder for which he was sentenced nearly forty years ago was made by Charles Parton (57), a market salesman of Bath, in an appeal for leniency at Southampton City Police Court on Saturday when he pleaded guilty to a charge of picking the pocket of a woman in Market Square and stealing a purse and money. Parton, a man of medium height and respectable appearance and wearing gold-rimmed glasses, appealed for consideration for the sake of his wife, an incurable consumptive, and young children. He told the Court he feared the Home Secretary would return him to penal servitude if he was sentenced. "For myself," he said, "I care nothing, my life is not worth living. My life has been a misery ever since my discharge from Dartmoor." Parton was sentenced to three months hard labour, as there were other convictions since his release from the life sentence to which sentence of death had been commuted. He was assured he was not likely to be sent back to penal servitude.

The last that was heard of Charles Parton was curiously enough published in the *Denton Journal* of Maryland on June 5th, 1930. The article reported that Parton was employed in the grounds of the Downside Benedictine Abbey, near Bath. "The man, now sixty, still protests his innocence as vigorously as ever, and says, 'I have found peace at last.' The monks, he adds, knowing his full history, befriended him when no one would employ him because of the stigma of prison."

Messrs. Robert Fletcher and Son

The business, formed in the early 1800s, originally traded as Ralph Crompton and Nephews, Bleachers and Papermakers, Stoneclough and Manchester. Paper was first made at Stoneclough in 1829. Robert Fletcher, John's father, entered the firm as a young man in his twenties in 1830 and his ability brought him to the notice of his employers and he became manager of the bleaching department and later manager of the whole mill. The Crompton family held him in high regard and Roger Crompton, the last of the founding brothers, left him both the principal trusteeship and the option of succeeding him in the firm. After the death of Roger Crompton, Robert Fletcher controlled the business with conspicuous ability and integrity for many years. He died at Vale House, Stoneclough, on May 17th, 1865, and was succeeded by his sons John and James Fletcher. They in turn were followed by their sons, John Robert Fletcher and James Fletcher. In 1897, the firm was incorporated as Robert Fletcher & Son Ltd. and in 1921, a second mill, at Greenfield, near Oldham, was opened which specialised in the manufacture of cigarette paper. Towards the late 1990s the two mills started to struggle and the company went into bankruptcy in 2001.

Victorian Manchester

The population of Manchester during Caminada's career was 300,000 to 350,000. Despite the growing wealth due to continued trade and commerce, prosperity lay in the hands of the very few. The working people, who were responsible for producing the wealth, lived, worked and died in conditions of the most desperate poverty and degradation.

Middle class attitudes to the plight of the working people were generally disparaging. The poor were regarded as an underclass with probable criminal tendencies, whose degradation was largely of their own doing. The poor were divided into "deserving" and "undeserving" groups. The former consisted of widows, orphans, the old and those incapable of work through illness, who were able to receive help through the Poor House system. The latter were the unemployed who were left entirely to their own devices.

Average wages in the nineteenth century were well below subsistence levels. A report from 1889 found that 61% of working men were defined as "very poor," with a weekly income of less than 4 shillings per week. 40% were "irregularly employed," holding positions such as warehousemen, labourers, store men and transport men. They were the first to be laid off in lean times, and no work literally meant no pay. They comprised the majority of the Smithfield Market labour force, the city's street sellers and hawkers, the building trade and domestic service. A large proportion of the irregularly employed were Irish immigrants. Half of those registered in the New Bridge Street Workhouse in the 1890s were Irish Catholics, and most lived in Ancoats. This area of the city, reported to be 40% Irish in the 1900 census, was probably the most deprived and the death spot of Manchester.

The dichotomy in living conditions between the rich and poor was thoroughly described by Caminada in Volume II of his memoirs.

> It is a truism that one half of the world does not know how the other half lives. In this great city we have, side by side with enormous wealth and luxury, an inconceivable amount of squalor, misery, degradation, and filthiness of life. There is scarcely any town on the continent where there is such a disparity of wealth and poverty. Those who want to see the city of Manchester ought to get up in the early morning. I do not think that any city in the world can boast of such warehouses and buildings – not even the metropolis itself – but anyone who stands among them in the middle of the day, when the streets are crowded with human life, has no time to observe this. Then, coming to other parts of the town, they would begin to see another phase of life. They would see curious, crawling, creeping figures, which they could scarcely believe to be human, slinking away in their rags. They would see lads and lassies, who had been homeless through the night, coming out of different passages where they had sought

temporary shelter. They would see forms flitting hither and thither – young girls in rags, upon whose faces are already imprinted the lowest forms of vice, and in which there was a kind of savage expression. There are two great streams of Manchester life, almost next door to each other, and yet as far apart as if one was at the North Pole and the other at the South. We can go through miles of streets where the respectable portion live, people in receipt of good wages, and where the districts themselves are not all unhealthy. But there is another picture. We can go down street after street where such a debased portion of humanity exists that we can scarcely have any idea of the kind of people who live there. They are people who have no certain employment or wages, and therefore their lives are uncertain from beginning to end. Sometimes they will make 16s. a week for several weeks, and then employment will stop, and they will have nothing whatever to fall back upon. Their houses are most wretchedly put together. They contain from four to six rooms, and there is street upon street and mile upon mile of these miserable houses. They are mere open lodging-houses. Instead of one house being inhabited by one family, we find not one family in each room but sometimes more – sleeping, eating and drinking together. It is impossible that there can be anything like decency, cleanliness, and modesty preserved. Yet all these people are hard-working. Some of the women are employed as fur-pullers, some work at shirt-making, some as tailoresses, and some go out charring. The children are sadly neglected, and many of the men are out of employment. Some of them pass half their time in the hospitals; others receive out-door relief and many are the victims of passing epidemics. It is not surprising that there is so much roughness of life, so much coarseness of thought, such assaults upon women, such neglect of children, such fighting, and such drunkenness. I yield to none in my advocacy of temperance, but I say there is a poverty in our midst which is not caused by drink. I do not say that there is not a great deal of poverty increased by drink, but where we have people living like this we must not be surprised if they are attracted to the glittering gin-palaces for their warmth and company. I often wonder that things are not ten times worse than they are.

Can one be surprised at Socialism existing? How is it possible for a man to support a wife and family on from 15s. to 18s. a week? How is it possible for a man under these conditions to put by for a rainy day? A man is a fool, says Mr Wiseacre, to marry under such circumstances. Experience is wise, but human nature is human nature all the world over. Many a man is saddled with a family before he sees his mistake, and youth does not stop to consider. But such an argument is rather a risky one for Mr Wiseacre, who is generally a capitalist taking advantage of this sort of thing. He

> knows a man cannot see his wife and children starve, and under the plea that half a loaf is better than none gives him starvation wages.

Workers tended to live near and around their places of work while the wealthy lived outside the city in their "garden suburbs." Workers' houses were "jerry" built in the absence of regulations and controls which only began to be brought in around 1875. The builder, normally the employer, would build so as to cram as many houses as possible in the space available. There were no water or other services, and no attempt to provide privacy of any kind. People worked in shifts and shared beds – up to a dozen people could share one bedroom. As many as 100 houses shared one toilet – a "privy," normally a deep hole dug in the corner of the yard, or a "midden," a heap against a wall. Houses were very damp in the absence of damp courses and double brick walls. Rain leeched through walls and damp rose up the walls.

The city had no policies for sewage disposal until late in the nineteenth century. Ashpits and communal cesspits were common which had to be emptied and carted away. They overflowed in rainy periods, often into cellars in which a large number of workers lived. Even by 1907 only about a third of the city's toilets were water closets and numerous middens and privies were still in use. Water closets, installed prior to 1870, simply ran directly into the Irwell, from which most people obtained their drinking water. Cholera was a common visitor in the summer.

In Volume I of his memoirs, Caminada vividly described such living conditions and the accommodations in which he was required to search for criminals.

> Manchester with all its great moral, and religious and political associations, its commercial enterprise recognized in every part of the world, and its corresponding wealth, has still its dark spots. Within an arrow's flight of the princely grandeur of its Town Hall may be seen many dwellings of misery and wretchedness.
>
> The exterior of one of those houses to which I propose to carry the mind of the reader will be a fair specimen of the rest. It presents a dingy face of crumbling brick, begrimed by the soot of years. The elevation consists of three storeys; the first two are lighted by windows which denote unmistakable antiquity, and multifarious are the methods employed to refute wind and rain admittance. Tattered garments, crowns of old hats, brown paper, and paper rendered brown by exposure, are all pressed into service of stopping a hole; and so varied are the contrivances utilized for this purpose, that the several windows are more suggestive of a rag merchant's establishment than a dwelling house of Christian England in the nineteenth century.
>
> On entering, we proceed along a lobby until we come to a room whence issues a babel of tongues, and in which a scene as extraordinary as can be

conceived presents itself. The apartment is full of men and women, though the former predominate. Some are seated on broken-backed chairs, or upon dilapidated stools ranged round a filthy table, most of the occupants eagerly devouring various kinds of messes, washed down by tea, coffee or beer. Others, again, are on their knees before the fire – one broiling a red herring; another, a slice of fat bacon. Some appear to have just left their beds, or, as is more probable, being obliged to quit them, have descended to the common room in a state of dishabille, and are proceeding to attach their tattered rags to their persons in the best way they can. Some of the women are patching garments, the primitive colour of which has long since vanished; others are endeavouring to make a stocking perform its duty one day more; and crouched on each side of the fire, such as it is, sit two thinly-clad creatures, whose bruised and disfigured faces are eloquent examples of the "bully's" brutal treatment which many of Eve's fallen and forlorn daughters have to endure.

Running along one side of the room is a dirty bench on which are a number of men smoking and drinking. The furniture is of the most meagre description, and consists of one table, some half-dozen broken-backed chairs, two stools and a bench. The walls are dotted with gaudily coloured prints, the subjects of which are mostly of a licentious nature. A few common ornaments are on the mantelpiece, the principal one being a large blue earthenware dog with a brown tail. The room reeks; the whole scene is squalid and cheerless; yet no sense of shame is visible on the countenance of the motley occupants.

Let the reader still follow me in imagination to view the same upstairs. The passages are narrow, the plaster broken off the walls in many places, the stairs weak and yielding to our footsteps. The room we enter contains four dirty rickety beds – mere pallets – the threadbare and ragged covering of which fails to conceal the creaking bedsteads and dirty straw mattresses beneath. The boards of the floor seem to have had no contact with the scrubbing brush for years, and we note the absence of all arrangements for personal cleanliness. On those beds rest, or rather restlessly lie, men and women of various types and ages, from the frowning confirmed felon to the innocent bastard babe. There lie old and young – grey-headed convict, wizened hag, infant and child of tender years – presenting a sickening picture of moral depravity; the atmosphere being nothing but a foetid composition of pestilential vapour emitted from filthy beds, dirty clothing, foul breath, and, worse than all, the presence of offensive matter in the room.

Doubtless the sad fate of most of those wretches is attributable to their own persistence in criminal wayward folly. Yea, they may not only have shaped their own crooked paths, but have willingly paced them until hardened in heart and reckless of consequence.

Yet how do you or I know what were the circumstances or environment of some of those unfortunate creatures? Much, no doubt, was due to the accident of birth. Had "Bill Sykes," the burglar, been born in a mansion and educated as befitted such a station in life, he might possibly have been a credit to the aristocracy of England; whereas had some scion of wealth sprung from the Charter Street gutter and inherited its vicious surroundings, he might have remained a tatterdemalion to this day.

Manchester was a very unhealthy place to live. A multitude of factory chimneys and coal burning domestic fires resulted in a permanent, acid-rain-drenched pall of smoke overhanging the city. Respiratory diseases such as bronchitis, influenza, pneumonia, asthma and industrial dust-related ailments, were at epidemic proportions. Pulmonary tuberculosis killed most citizens. The highest death rates were in the inner city areas of Ancoats, Chorlton-on-Medlock, Hulme and Ardwick.

Surveys carried out during the nineteenth century all told the same story: long working hours and poor wages, dangerous working conditions, unsanitary dwellings, no health provisions, high infant mortality rates and short life expectancy. A typical working day was at least fourteen hours long in the absence of regulations. Life expectancy was directly proportional to wealth and the life expectancy of a working man in 1870 could be as little as seventeen years.

The city's slow rate of conversion to water closets and sewage disposal were the cause of an extraordinarily high infant mortality rate. In addition to the threat from backyard middens, other causes of infant mortality were insect-borne germs, inadequate washing facilities, poor food hygiene and a very poor diet.

Victorian Manchester was also a hotbed of conmen, vice and depravity, and Deansgate, on the west side of the city centre, was regarded as one of the most dangerous places in the country with a nationwide reputation for lawlessness. Caminada was not at all surprised that the drugging of John Fletcher could take place in the Deansgate and old Market Place region. The area was peppered with pubs and cases of drugging for the purposes of robbery were frequent. He described the area in Volume I of his autobiography.

> The neighbourhood of Deansgate also was the rendezvous of thieves and was a very hot-bed of social iniquity and vice. The women of the locality were of the most degraded class, and their chief victims were drunken men, collier lads, and country "flats," whom they picked up and rifled with impunity.
>
> Such places as the "Dog and Rat," the "Red, White and Blue," the "Old Ship," the "Pat M'Carthy," the "Green Man," and other equally notorious places were then in full swing as licensed beerhouses. Passing these the

pedestrian's ear would be arrested by the sound of music proceeding from mechanical organs, accompanied sometimes with drums and tambourines. On entering the premises he would find a number of youths and girls assembled in a room furnished with a few wooden forms and tables. The women generally lived upon the premises, the proprietor of the den often adding to his income by the proceeds of their shame. Some rude attempt would probably be made at an indecent song by a half-drunken girl for the edification of some collier lads, who were the chief victims of these haunts, but her voice would be drowned by the incessant quarrelling and obscene language of her companions.

Many places of this kind were carried on which had no licence whatever for the sale of intoxicating liquors, and there were other noted "cribs" (houses) where intoxicants could always be had when public houses were closed. There were also well-known beerhouses which did nearly the whole of their business during prohibited hours, all sorts of poisonous stuff being sold to the public under the guise of beer or spirits. Men were employed in these places for the purpose of watching for the police, and warning landlords of their approach.

"Bullies," or "Coshers" were another kind of criminal who preyed upon the community. They got hold of some girl whom they compelled to lead a loose life, and when she had accosted and decoyed her victim to some convenient place, the "Cosher" would put in an appearance, and rob him of all the valuables he possessed, in some cases garroting him, while, should any opposition be offered, the victim would be severely beaten.

Caminada described the quality of the entertainment in a typical Deansgate pub in more detail in Volume II of his memoirs. At this time public houses were allowed to stay open for twenty-one hours, from 4 am to 1 am the next morning. A considerable amount of time was consequently spent entertaining the criminal classes and the result was very poor quality performances.

> In some of the public houses in the neighbourhood, what is called a "free and easy" is held. The rooms are generally crammed to suffocation, and there is some difficulty in obtaining a seat. The atmosphere is most vile; everyone smokes, and how anyone can sing in such a place is surprising. If you look around you will find that the company is composed of all kinds of people, from the "grave and reverend seignor" to the beardless youth. All have glasses of something to drink before them, and the waiters ply their trade briskly.
>
> A young man sits at one end of the room playing a piano, whilst another who sits near him acts as chairman. After a tune the chairman

gets up and announces that Mr So-and-So "will oblige," at which the company expresses its pleasure by knocking their glasses on the table. Mr So-and-So now takes his stand near the pianist, and, after humming over the air to him, treats his audience to one of those patriotic songs which hurl defiance at the foreigner.

From an intellectual point of view there is nothing very elevating about the performance; but this is not intended. Large salaries are realized by men and women who contrive with scarcely any effort to gratify the tastes of that portion of the public which frequents these places. Many ingenious individuals can earn more money by blacking their faces than any barrister or physician can make by the laborious pursuit of his learned calling. Anyone who is able to sing a comic song, and accompany it with appropriate contortions of visage, seems to be on the highway to prosperity. The closer a man or a woman can imitate a negro minstrel or an idiot, the more certain is he or she of popularity.

The songs of these music rooms are the most arrant nonsense ever concocted; yet people crowd day after day to hear them. The singers, especially the women, are rather commonplace or extremely bad, and for months do not make the least alteration to their repertoire. The woman who was squalling *Maggie Murphy's Home* twelve months ago is probably doing so now with a voice not improved by constant exercise in a hot and stifling atmosphere.

Strange to say, the most popular of the singers, as certainly the most objectionable and offensive, are the female comiques. They have only to adorn their faces with a beard or moustache, or wear their dresses without being particular as to the length, to be sure of encores. To see a fat woman waddle about the stage in a long beard and a short dress is a spectacle the charms of which must be inscrutable to those who have not been partially reared in music halls.

Turning to the criminal justice system of the late Victorian era, Caminada also offered his views in this subject. For example, in Volume I he expressed sympathy with some of the wretches who appeared in court and seemed to put the blame fairly and squarely on the unfairness of society.

I have often heard remarks passed when some poor dejected looking, ill-clad fellow has been brought up in court. "What a bad looking fellow that is!" whilst a far worse criminal, of greater danger to society, whose friends have been able to provide him with clothing to make a respectable appearance in the dock, often excites the sympathy and pity of the onlookers.

Drink, no doubt, is responsible for many of these people making their appearance in gaol; but surrounded as they are by a vast desert of bricks and mortar, with nothing except the public house in their midst to enliven them, or to arouse pleasant emotions, is it to be wondered that women become drunk and untidy, and that men desert their homes for the public house, become selfish and brutal towards their families, or that they and their children recruit the criminal classes? As we sow so shall we reap. Wherever the ruling classes neglect their duties towards those over whom they are placed, they must take the consequences. If the rich man's horses and dogs are better housed, trained and cared for than the children of the poor, then the dogs and horses will be more tractable and docile than the children.

Nevertheless, in the conclusion of Volume II of his memoirs, Caminada gave his opinion, a very positive one, on the quality of the justice system in place at the time.

I wish to place on record my conviction as to the absolute purity and fairness which attend the administration of justice in this country. Now and again a magistrate, or even a judge of the High Court, may take an erroneous view of a case, and be led to a decision which is either too severe or too lenient. But I do not hesitate to assert that the judicial bench and the magistracy are alike above suspicion, and for generations the local judiciary of Manchester have enjoyed a reputation that has been admittedly spotless. I have also been very favourably impressed by the efforts of the magistrates to sift and weigh evidence before or against prisoners; and the pains which are, on every occasion, taken to elicit the truth cannot fail to inspire popular confidence.

He was not so generous when offering his opinions of sentencing policies, as discussed in Volume I of his memoirs. Caminada considered that sentences for criminal offences were particularly punitive and not conducive to reform.

I desire to say that in the treatment of our criminals I should like to see a more uniform mode of sentencing prisoners adopted. I have often stood by when men have been sentenced to terms of penal servitude which have filled me with sorrow, because I have been convinced that in many cases the sentence meant either a criminal death or insanity; for, astounding as the statement may appear, I have never yet known a man or woman return from a long term of penal servitude in their rational mind; and yet in all probability the criminal had never in the course of his or her life a single chance of getting out of the circumstances in which he or she was born, breathing through poverty an air of temptation.

A few years ago it was the common conversation of residents in criminal neighbourhoods to talk of who was for "big fulley" (assizes), or "little fulley" (sessions), as to whether they would get "legged" (sent to penal servitude) for five, seven, ten or more years. I have known a man to be sentenced to fourteen years for stealing two pence; another to ten years for stealing a pair of boots, hat, and linen jacket, of the total value of 12s.; two men to seven years for stealing a halfpenny; whilst another rogue was sentenced to twelve months imprisonment for stealing £4,000; and another bound over to appear when called upon for stealing £100. I could go into this matter if it were necessary, but I will leave the reader to form his own judgment as to whether short sentences would not serve in cases of this kind. As long as our system of punishment for the repression of crime is accompanied by degradation, it will tend more to foster criminal propensities than to remove them. Degradation strengthens evil propensities, prevents repentance, and renders reform almost impossible. How comes it that the worst criminals are those who have undergone the most imprisonment? Punishment is not correction, and degradation only brutalizes human nature. The freed prisoner is a pestiferous thing which society detests and abhors. He therefore goes from you to your enemies. There he is welcomed; there he is helped; and there he is strengthened for greater evil.

PART ONE
THE JUDICIAL ENQUIRY

CHAPTER I

The Coroner's Court, Day One, March 1st

On the morning of Friday, March 1st, 1889, the Deputy Coroner for Manchester, Mr. Sidney Smelt, opened an inquest at the Coroner's Court, St John Street, into the death of Mr. John Fletcher of Southport. Fletcher was found in a dying condition in a cab in one of the streets of Manchester on Tuesday, February 26th. The circumstances of the case had excited profound and widespread interest; as head of the firm of Messrs. Robert Fletcher and Son, paper manufacturers, the deceased gentleman was well known in commercial circles.

Mr Walter Hocklin watched the proceeds on behalf of Fletcher's relatives and the Manchester police authorities were represented by Mr Superintendent Meade and Chief Detective Inspector Caminada.

Smelt opened the inquiry by summarizing the facts known. "The facts of this case are very short. It appears that Mr Fletcher had been at the Mitre Hotel by the Cathedral and left there with a young fellow at present unknown. They took a cab to the Three Arrows public house in Deansgate and then again towards Stretford. While on route the cabman stopped, found the young fellow had disappeared and that there was something wrong with Fletcher who also appeared to have had his pockets turned-out. Fletcher was then driven to the Infirmary and found to be dead upon arrival.

"An examination was made of the body and at my direction a *post-mortem* examination was made by one of the surgeons of the Infirmary, and the stomach was sent to Mr Estcourt, the city analyst, for the purpose of being subjected to analysis. I have a letter form Mr Estcourt, I am sorry to say, stating that the analysis will not be ready for the inquest today, so an adjournment will be necessary.

"What you have to inquire into is the cause of death, and whether anyone was to blame for it. If upon careful analysis of the contents of the stomach and as a result of the *post-mortem* examination, generally it should be perfectly clear that Mr Fletcher's death was due to natural causes, there should be no necessity for you to go into all the details about whether or not the man had been robbed. Of course these are matters for another court to inquire into."

Evidence was first adduced as to identification. Mr Robert Fletcher, of Stoneclough, near Bolton, was a nephew of the deceased. He stated the deceased was a widower, fifty years of age and resided at Elmhurst, Albert Road, Birkdale, Southport. He described his uncle as a big stout man about 6 ft. in height, but during the last twelve or fifteen months he had gotten thinner. Robert Fletcher last saw his Uncle alive about a quarter-past one in the afternoon on Tuesday, February 26th, at his place of business, Messrs. Robert Fletcher and Son, paper manufacturers, Cannon Street, Manchester. On leaving the office the deceased remarked that he was attending the sale of a mill at the Mitre Hotel at half-past four, would not go back to Southport that night and would see his nephew next morning at the mill in Stoneclough. At about half-past eleven on Wednesday morning Robert Fletcher heard that his uncle was at the Infirmary and subsequently went to see him there the same day to identify his body. When John Fletcher left the office on Tuesday, his nephew testified that he had a sum of money in a wash-leather purse and was wearing a valuable gold watch.

Hocklin added, "The company cashier is here who gave him a sum of money on the 26th."

George Wild, living at Uplands, Whitefield, said he was at the Mitre Hotel on Tuesday last, at the sale of a mill. He did not see John Fletcher at the sale, but saw him afterwards around a quarter-past five. Wild spoke to him for about five minutes, noticed he was well under the influence of drink, and then left him in conversation with two friends. At the time Fletcher was wearing his gold watch and guard and gold-rimmed spectacles. He did not say anything about his movements or where he intended to go. Wild added that he thought that Fletcher, "Openly flaunted his wealth a little too much and was an obvious target for thieves or pickpockets," and that, "Fletcher was a genial sort of man whom I had often met at the Mitre Hotel. He was in the habit of going also to Sinclair's and to the Tower Hotel. On this particular day he was very jubilant over his success in being elected to the County Council."

William Hall, of Diggle, Saddleworth, stated that he was with George Wild on Tuesday, and saw the deceased at the Mitre Hotel at around five o'clock in the afternoon, just after the sale finished. Fletcher was alone and Hall remained with him for twenty to twenty-five minutes. Fletcher left to go to Sinclair's oyster rooms and Hall and his father intended to follow. They did not however end up going and Hall never saw the deceased again. Hall was unable to confirm if Fletcher went to Sinclairs' oyster rooms or not. He confirmed that Fletcher had both watch and money, for he saw him change a sovereign paying for three glasses of claret for friends and a glass of sherry for himself. The deceased had been drinking and was somewhat "elevated," but was quite sensible and had been talking about City Council matters.

Fletcher intended on going to Sinclair's Oyster Bar after leaving the Mitre Hotel.

Edward Lait, of 17, Mary Street, Strangeways, said he had a place for the sale of dried fish and game at 10, Victoria Street, adjoining Sinclair's oyster rooms. He knew Fletcher well and often saw him in Victoria Street near his stall. He did confirm having seen Fletcher on Tuesday evening standing in the street close to his stall at about 6:40. He was in the company of a young man and the two stood talking together for two to three minutes. Shortly before, he had seen Fletcher alone, coming through the Shambles from the direction of Kenyon's (the Wellington Inn) public house in Market Place. Lait did not notice Fletcher leave, he only saw him standing in the street. Fletcher was very much the worse for drink and was wearing his spectacles. Lait added that Fletcher was very genial and good tempered, and agreeable to everybody. He had seen Mr Fletcher, "a little over the line" before.

Edward Lait observed Fletcher walking towards his stall from the direction of Kenyon's & the Wellington Inn.

Police Constable William Jakeman next deposed as follows. "About twenty minutes to seven on Tuesday evening I noticed an elderly gentleman, who I later discovered was Mr Fletcher, in the company of a young man around the Cromwell monument, Victoria Street, about half-way between Cateaton Street and the Cathedral steps. I heard the older of the two say, 'Get me a cab,' or words to that effect. The young man held up his finger to a cabman on the stand in the centre of the street and presently a cab drew up. Both men climbed into the cab which was driven away in the direction of Deansgate.

"A little later, the cab returned to where it had departed from and the cabman told me that the young man had jumped out of the cab whilst it was travelling along Stretford Road and that he could do nothing with the older gentleman. The cabman was hoping that I might know something of his passengers since I saw them get into his cab and wanted me to help him get his fare. I looked in the cab, saw the elderly man and commented, 'I think he has been having a lot of drink since he was here before.' He was sitting in a stooping position at the far corner of the cab. I spoke to him but got no answer. I then got into the cab, raised his head and placed it against the back of the cab. The old gentleman's eyes were open but he appeared to be quite unconscious.

"Assuming that drink was the cause of the insensibility, I said to the cabman, 'We had better go to the Albert Street police station.' I then instructed the cabman to take the deceased and myself there, climbed into the cab and closed the door.

The Cromwell monument where Fletcher and Parton hailed the cab.

The cabman drove along Deansgate and turned right into Blackfriars Street. Just as the cab turned left into the Parsonage, I became anxious about the man's condition, had the cab stopped, and examined him more carefully. I reported to the cabman, 'This man is seriously ill, drive straight to the Infirmary.' The cab drove back along Blackfriars Street, into St Mary's Gate and then Market Street to the Infirmary at Piccadilly. On reaching the Infirmary he was at once admitted and attended to by one of the physicians, who pronounced life to be extinct. In my opinion he died just as we were crossing the Infirmary yard at which point he emitted a deep sigh from his throat."

The constable did not notice anything strange in the cab but there was a little white foam on Fletcher's lips which he wiped away. Also, his waistcoat was raised disclosing his shirt and there was no watch or guard.

In response to a question by Smelt inquiring if he later examined the deceased's clothing, Jakeman responded, "Yes, at the Infirmary. I found two pairs of spectacles, gold-rimmed, one in a case and one loose in the inside breast pocket of his overcoat. There was also a small gold pencil-case in one of the waistcoat pockets, a bunch of keys in one of the trouser pockets and gold studs in the shirt. I found no papers, except an envelope with some figures on that no one could make out, and a cheque book."

Jakeman wrote a rough description of the young man in his notebook on the same evening when he saw him hail the cab at the Cathedral stand. He wrote, "Age twenty-two years; dressed in a dark brown suit and a pot hat and about 5ft. 2ins. or 5ft. 3ins. in height; fresh looking; no side whiskers or moustache."

Harry Goulding, cabman, was the next called. He lived at 31, Bow Street, Milton Street, Broughton. "About 6:40 on Tuesday evening I was sitting on the Cromwell monument stand when I was hailed by a young man who was with an elderly gentleman, who afterwards turned out to be Mr Fletcher. I walked the cab to the side of the footpath and the two men got in. As I was closing the door behind them, the young man said, 'Drive to the Three Arrows.' I drove down Deansgate to the public house named at the corner of Deansgate and St Mary's Street, and there the two stayed about twenty minutes, entering by the side door in St Mary's Street.

"I waited outside with the cab and had a smoke. Very few people went in and out of the Three Arrows whilst I waited there. I saw them seated in one of the rooms at a table with their backs to the wall. I did not notice anyone else at the table. They had two glasses in front of them, and they appeared to be engaged in conversation. I had just finished my pipe when the two came out. The older gentleman came out first, walked steadily and got into the cab without assistance. The younger man followed immediately and also got into the cab. He was also pretty steady and in no way intoxicated. I closed the door behind them. The old gentleman did not speak to me, but I did speak to the young man who next told me to go to, '43, Stretford Road.'

"I drove down Deansgate, along Peter Street and Oxford Street to All Saints' church, into Cavendish Street and onto Stretford Road. At, or near, the junction of Stretford Road and Cambridge Street I had to drive slowly and then walk with the horse, because of a publicity procession for a show then exhibiting in Manchester called 'Mexican Joes.' There was a great crowd of people on both sides of the street and in the roadway. After the procession had passed I drove on again for about a hundred yards. A working man then called to inform me that a passenger had just jumped out of my cab and run off. I then noticed that the door to the cab was open. I stopped the cab, got down from the box and found the young fellow had disappeared.

"The older gentleman was still in the cab bent over with his head down on the seat he was facing. I got into the cab and with the assistance of the working man who had called the situation to my attention, tried to raise him up. He seemed to be in a stupid, intoxicated condition, and all he said was, 'Go away and leave me alone.' To get away from the crowd and with the working man inside the cab, I drove on and turned left into Renshaw Street and left again into Boundary Street heading back to Oxford Street. On getting into Boundary Street, I stopped and tried again to rouse the old gentleman. Failing in my efforts I told the working man I would need no further assistance and I drove back to Oxford Street and retraced my steps to the cab stand where the two men had got into the cab in the first instance. I there saw the same policeman who was on the footpath when I was first hailed, and with him I afterwards drove to the Infirmary."

Goulding described the young man as, "Fresh looking, clean shaven, no whiskers or moustache, about 5ft. 3in. in height, and was dressed in a brownish suit with a billycock hat."

At this point, one of the jurors asked the cabman, "Do you not think it would have been better for you to have driven to the All Saints' police station in the first instance?"

Goulding replied, "I thought I would go back to the place whence I came."

Smelt added, "No doubt it would have been better to have driven to the nearest police station, but the cabman had no idea that the man was ill, and he was desirous of getting his fare."

The juror added, "It might have been the means of saving the man's life if the cabman had gone to the nearest police station."

"Well, possibly, but we don't always think for the best," responded Smelt.

Harry Smith, employed at 43, Stretford Road, next deposed that he had seen the body of the deceased at the Infirmary. His employer had never had any dealings with Mr Fletcher, and he could suggest no reason as to why he should plan a visit to their shop. The shop was closed at night and no one slept on the premises.

Mary Frost, landlady of the Three Arrows was next called. "Fletcher, accompanied by a young man, came into my hotel about half-past six o'clock on Tuesday evening. I served them with drink in the smoke-room. Fletcher ordered the drinks – two bitter beers. I served him, and he paid for them. He tendered a shilling, and that was all the money I saw he had. They were not in the house long, only had one drink each and did not seem to talk much to each other."

Caminada stated, "That is all the police evidence, with the exception of the medical men."

Smelt reported, "Mr Estcourt, the public analyst, will not be ready to give evidence before Monday. In view of that I think it would be better not to take the evidence of Dr Reynolds, the resident medical officer at the Manchester Royal Infirmary, today. In fact I think he would rather wait for Mr Estcourt's analysis." Dr Reynolds agreed and the Inquest was then adjourned until Monday afternoon at two o'clock.

CHAPTER II

The City Police Court, First Appearance, March 2nd

In the City Police Court, Minshull Street, on Saturday morning, March 2nd, the magistrates on the bench were the Stipendiary (Mr Francis Headlam), Mr James Parlane, and Mr R. A. Armitage.

The circumstances under which John Fletcher met his death absorbed much public attention. The outcome of the inquest on Friday was somewhat disappointing, but excitement was created on Saturday by the announcement that the police had arrested a young man and that there was strong reason for believing that he was the individual who accompanied Mr Fletcher in the cab on Tuesday evening.

Despite the excitement, there were surprisingly few people in the City Police Court when the prisoner, Charles Parton, was placed in the dock. The fact that an arrest had been made had not become generally known. The prisoner seemed perfectly cool and collected.

Chief Detective Inspector Caminada opened proceedings and stated, "About half-past twelve this morning I, in company with two other detective officers, apprehended the prisoner at 12, Moore Street, Rochdale Road. I took him to the Detective Office, and this morning I placed him with seven other men. He was identified by the cabman as being the person that he drove from the Cathedral steps to the Three Arrows and to Stretford Road on Tuesday night last in company with the gentleman who is now deceased.

"A second cabman, who drove him from a beer house in Higher Chatham Street to Oldham Road, picked him out from the same number of men. The prisoner was also identified by a woman in that beerhouse who saw him place a handful of money on the table and by a man from the same house whom he gave sixpence to bring a cab. He was identified by Sergeant Allinson, of the detective force, who saw him in the cab driving to Oldham Road, and finally by a police officer who was standing near him in Victoria Street when he entered a cab and took it to the Three Arrows."

Caminada continued, "I then reminded him to be cautious how he answered and to take care and not to respond rashly. I charged him with having stolen on Tuesday night last from the person of one John Fletcher a gold watch and chain, valued at £120, and a sum of money, the amount of which is at present unknown. I also charged him on suspicion with having caused the death of John Fletcher, on Tuesday night last between half-past six and half-past seven

THE CITY POLICE COURT, FIRST APPEARANCE, MARCH 2ND

o'clock. In answer to that he said, 'I was at home at my tea before six o'clock. I had been to the course.'

"I now ask your Worship to grant a remand, and to remand the prisoner to some day next week. We want, if possible, to produce him before the Coroner on Monday. The inquest has been adjourned until then."

The prisoner was not represented and Headlam asked him, "Do you want to ask any questions of the witness?"

"No, I have no questions. I know nothing about this affair. I have a dozen witnesses that can prove I was at a benefit at a quarter to seven," replied Parton.

Caminada asked whether their Worships would care to hear any other witnesses?

Headlam responded, "Certainly we would."

PC Jakeman and cabdriver Henry Goulding repeated the evidence they had given before the Coroner's Court on March 1st. When Goulding had completed his deposition, Headlam asked, "Was Fletcher drunk when he entered the cab after drinking in the Three Arrows?"

"No," replied Goulding.

"Then how did he get drunk in the cab?"

"I don't know. He got into the cab without any assistance."

"Then you left him at the police station?"

"No. The bobby looked at him in the Parsonage and said, 'I think there's something the matter with him; you had better take him to the Infirmary as soon as you can.' He got inside and I drove to the Infirmary. I saw another policeman at the bottom of Market Street, and I told him to get inside, as his mate wanted him particular. The officer did so, and when we reached there it was found that the gentleman was dead."

Headlam asked, "Are you certain this is the young man?"

"Yes, I am certain that is the young man," replied Goulding.

Caminada then added, "There are two or three other witnesses I would ask your worships to hear. This is new evidence not heard on the first day of the inquest."

Emily Pearson, who was then called, said, "I am housekeeper to my father, Andrew Holt, who keeps a public house at 39, Higher Chatham Street, called the York Minster. I was in the beerhouse dressing upstairs on Tuesday evening, and on coming down I found a young man in the bar parlour. It was just short of half-past seven. My daughter had served the young man with a small soda, and he asked for

Parton's destination after jumping out of the cab was the York Minster.

a little milk. I sent my daughter into the kitchen for the milk and when she brought it, poured it into a glass. He asked my daughter what she charged and she said nothing. He said he would pay a penny and put his hand in his pocket. He could only find a halfpenny in copper. I then left the room, but believe he got change and paid the penny. When I went back in a cabman had arrived. The young man then took out his gold watch and looking at the clock asked if it was right. My father said it was, and he then shook hands with me and my father and bade us good night."

Headlam asked, "Is this the young man?"

The Manchester Courier and Lancashire Advertiser, *Saturday, March 9, 1889.*

"That is the young man," replied Pearson.

William Coleman, cabdriver, thirty-one, Higher Ormond Street, then gave evidence. He deposed, "I was called to the beerhouse in Higher Chatham Street by a man who said a gentleman wanted me inside. I went in and saw a young man who asked me what I would like to drink. I said I didn't mind a ginger ale. He said alright and asked me, 'What will you drive me to New Cross for?' I said eighteen pence. He said it was very reasonable. He had some conversation with the master of the house about a soda and milk, and there was some talk about only having a halfpenny in change, and that he would have to change a sixpence. He got change from the master of the house, and in another minute said, 'We will go.' I said, 'All right,' and we went outside. I got on the front, and he also got up. He had been telling me that he had been in London, and I thought that was the custom there. I drove along Higher Chatham Street, into Cavendish Street and onto Oxford Street.

When we got to Oxford Street he wanted to drive but I refused to let him. He then got all in a shiver and I gave him my rug and suggested he get inside the cab. When near Clarendon Street, I stopped and he did get inside. When he was inside he told me to pull up at Jack Rook's. I drove along Oxford Street to St Peter's Square, then onto Mosley Street to Piccadilly. At Piccadilly I took Oldham Street up to New Cross. When I got to the Cross he wanted me to pull up, but I wouldn't until we got to Rook's, that's the Locomotive Inn, in the first street off Oldham Road, just up Henry Street."

Headlam then asked, "Mr. Coleman, did you see the young man with a watch?"

The witness responded, "At the York Minster I saw the watch. It was a gold watch with an oval glass and a white face with a second finger on. It had a long curb which he had hanging from one of the top buttons of his waistcoat."

Headlam next addressed Caminada, "Is the man who changed the money for the prisoner here?"

"No, I couldn't get him today; he had to take charge of the beerhouse. He will be available Tuesday."

Thomas Hibbs of 52 Ashover Street, Hyde Road, describing himself as a housekeeper, said he got a cab and took it to the York Minster about twenty-five past seven on Tuesday night. He there saw Charles Parton and the landlord, Andrew Holt. After he got there Parton stayed about five minutes. Hibbs went for a cab for the prisoner in Higher Chatham Street and got 6d for the job. He opened the cab door but Parton would not get in and said he would ride outside. He was driven up Chatham Street. He next saw Parton on Saturday morning at the Town Hall and had no doubt about him being the same person.

That completed the evidence against Parton. The prisoner was remanded until Monday and was immediately removed in a cab to the Town Hall in the charge of Caminada and other officers.

CHAPTER III

The City Police Court, Second Appearance, March 4th

On the morning of Monday, March 4th, Parton was brought before the magistrates, at the City Police Court, for the second time. He was previously remanded until this day on a charge of robbing John Fletcher, and also on suspicion of causing his death. The court was crowded with spectators. The magistrates on the bench on this occasion were the Stipendiary (Mr Headlam), Mr Alderman King, Mr James Parlane, Mr R. A. Armitage and Colonel Haworth. Mr. William Burton, solicitor, had by this time been appointed to appear on behalf of the prisoner.

Chief Detective Inspector Caminada said, "The prisoner, your worship, was brought before the Court on Saturday last and remanded until today. Since then, sir, he has been identified by a chemist in Liverpool, as having on Monday last, stolen a bottle containing one pound weight of chloral, and that is a charge that will be brought against him when he is brought up finally before the court. He is further to be charged, in a totally separate incident, with having on December 28th last, stolen from another person, a silver watch worth £9 and about 13s. 6d. in cash, by administering to him some drug in a public house. I will ask your worship if you will please to grant a remand for today, as we want to produce the prisoner before the Coroner later today."

Headlam stated, "I thought he had been there?"

Caminada responded, "No, sir; the jury do not sit until two o'clock."

"How long will you want to remand for? When will you be ready?"

"We shall not be ready for a little time, but if you will grant a remand until tomorrow, we shall be ready to finish it then. I am instructed by the Chief Constable to say that Mr William Cobbett has been retained by the police to prosecute, and we do not want to bring him into the case until we are quite ready."

At this point, Burton addressing Headlam, stated, "I am instructed on behalf of the prisoner to say that he has a complete answer to any charge that has been brought against him, and that will be a ground for my applying to you to see if you could see your way to grant him bail."

Headlam replied, "Certainly not. I could not in a case of this kind. It may be a case of mistaken identity, that I cannot say anything about, but I cannot grant bail."

Burton responded, "I have not heard the case before, therefore I made the application as instructed by the prisoner."

The prisoner was formally remanded until March 5th and removed in custody of the police.

CHAPTER IV

The Coroner's Court, Day Two, March 4th

The Coroner's inquiry into Mr John Fletcher's death resumed at 2 pm on Monday, March 4th, at the Courthouse, before the Deputy City Coroner, Mr Sidney Smelt.

The arrest of Parton, and the important evidence as to his identity given at the City Police Court on Saturday morning and in the earlier part of the day, had aroused intense interest in the proceedings. A vast assemblage of men, women and youths thronged the roadway in front of the small court, and all available space within the building was occupied long before resumption of the inquest. At the outset of the proceedings the Deputy Coroner gave directions for the court to be cleared of all persons except those directly interested in the case and representatives of the press. This was done for the purpose of preventing the air, which had become somewhat foul, from getting still further depressing. The clearance, however, had only a temporary effect, for very speedily the Court became filled again.

As before, Mr. William Hocklin watched on behalf of the relatives of the deceased and Detective Chief Inspector Caminada represented the police authorities. On this occasion Mr William Burton appeared on behalf of the prisoner. Charles Parton was present during the proceedings dressed in a neat tweed suit.

The inquiry on Friday was adjourned at the point where the medical evidence was to come.

The first witness called was Mr Phillip Estcourt, Fellow of the Chemical Society, who deposed as follows; "I act as clerk for Mr Charles Estcourt, the analyst for the Manchester Corporation, and I received on Thursday, February 28th at 4:30 from Police Constable Valentine two jars sealed and labelled. The first was labeled, 'Contents of upper part of small intestines; Mr Fletcher's case.' The second and larger jar was labelled, 'Stomach and contents of Mr. Fletcher.' These I locked up and delivered to Mr Charles Estcourt in the same condition as that in which I received them. On Sunday March 3rd, I went to the Infirmary and at twelve o'clock received from Dr Reynolds a jar sealed and labelled, 'Fluid from the abdominal cavity, removed Friday, March 1st, at 2 p.m. Case of Mr Fletcher.'"

Mr Charles Estcourt, City Analyst, was next examined. He said, "I am a Fellow of the Chemical Society, Fellow of the Institute of Chemistry, Fellow of the Society of Public Analysts, and Analyst to the City of Manchester and several other boroughs. I received on the days mentioned the jars as described by the last witness, my son, and I have since examined the contents. I examined them particularly with a view to ascertain whether or not chloroform of hydrate or chloral were present. The jars themselves had an alcoholic smell, and I could detect no smell of chloroform in any of them. I therefore submitted the contents to an exceedingly delicate process by which chloral hydrate is decomposed if present. The decomposition results in the production of chloroform, which if present even in very minute quantities, can now be detected. I did detect a trace of chloroform, under such conditions as proved it had been derived from chloral hydrate. That is the result of my analysis."

Smelt asked Estcourt, "Was it an appreciable quantity?"

"It was appreciable by chemical tests distinctly," replied Estcourt.

"But nothing more than a trace?"

"Nothing more than a trace".

"Was it such a trace as you would be able to discover in beer or whisky? I mean, is it one of the constituent parts of beer or whisky?"

"It is not".

"If you analyzed whisky or beer or any alcoholic drink you would have no such results?"

"No I should not. No such results would be attained by applying the same tests to beer or whiskey. It is undoubtedly a foreign substance".

Under cross-examination by Burton, Estcourt was then asked, "When you first examined the jars you noticed a smell of alcoholic liquor?"

"I did," replied Estcourt

"Could you from the analysis you made pronounce any opinion as to the habits of the deceased?"

"I could not".

"Would you undertake to say that chloral or chloroform was not present in spirits when analyzed?"

"I should say they were not present. I will give you an illustration. The third jar, like the others, had a strong alcoholic smell, and contained the fluid from the abdominal cavity. When submitted to the same tests as the others it gave no trace of chloral or chloroform."

Burton changed tack and continued, "Were the intestines inflamed?"

Smelt interrupted, "That is more a question for the doctor." He then asked Estcourt, "Can you tell us anything about the effects of chloral?"

"It is very rapidly absorbed and is often undetected when death ensues after a brief period."

John Hampden-Barker M.D. (Victoria University) deposed as follows. "I was up to Friday last, house physician at the Manchester Royal Infirmary and was on duty when Mr Fletcher was brought there. He was then dead. Death had only taken place a very short time previously. I examined his mouth and nose and found no sign of any irritation or irritant poison. He was very pale. I examined his mouth with the object of detecting any unusual smell, but could only detect the smell of alcohol.

THE CORONER'S COURT, DAY TWO, MARCH 4TH

A few minutes later I examined the breath for prussic acid, applying chemical tests to the mouth, but failed to find any trace of such poison. I could say from his appearance that morphia and strychnine might be eliminated from the cause of death. He appeared to have died from syncope, due to failure of the heart's action, but I could not find anything in the condition of the body to account for syncope."

Under cross-examination, Hampden-Barker was asked by Burton, "Could syncope be produced by excessive amounts of alcohol?"

Hampden-Parker responded, "The taking of a large quantity of drink might produce syncope in a man troubled with heart disease. I have known cases of persons dying from syncope who have been inebriated, especially if they were subject to heart disease. The deceased smelled very strongly of alcohol, and there was no other smell present. If I had not had further information, I could not have said what was the cause of death."

Burton followed, "Would you have come to the conclusion that he had died from an excessive drinking bout?"

"I could not give an opinion," replied Hampden-Barker.

The next witness was Ernest Reynolds, M.D. (London) and Member of the Royal College of Physicians. He stated, "I am the resident medical officer at the Manchester Royal Infirmary. I first examined the body of Mr Fletcher at ten o'clock on Wednesday morning last, in order to detect, if possible, any odour in the breath. I only smelled alcohol. I made a *post-mortem* examination, assisted by Dr Hampden-Barker, at three o'clock in the afternoon of the same day. There were no marks externally that would at all account for death, there being only three very old scars on the left shin and bruises on the left knee. Internally, the body was very well nourished. On opening the body there was a very strong smell of alcohol, but of nothing else. The bag around the heart was normal. The heart itself was large, but considering the size of the body I should say not unhealthily so. It was somewhat contracted on both sides and contained a little perfectly fluid blood. In fact the blood throughout the body was everywhere fluid. I found no clots whatever.

Smelt asked, "Has that any significance?"

"Yes, it is said to have significance by certain authorities."

Reynolds continued, "The heart was quite healthy except for a few very small patches of degeneration on the mitral valve and a few similar patches were seen on the aorta, the principal blood vessel leading from the heart. All the valves of the heart were in good working order. The larynx, trachea and bronchi were slightly congested, but there was no disease, and nothing but the smell of alcohol about them. The lungs were also slightly congested, but otherwise quite healthy. They, too, smelled of alcohol when cut into. The right pleura showed signs of old inflammation; the left being healthy. The mouth, tongue and gullet were healthy, showing no signs of irritation. The stomach contained about a gill of brownish fluid, of the consistency of gruel. This smelled strongly of beer, but I could not detect any other smell. The stomach wall was slightly congested and showed several small hemorrhages in the substance. The rest of the intestines as far down almost as the rectum contained gruelly fluid, smelling strongly of alcohol. I could make nothing of this fluid except that it appeared due to a very liquid form of food the deceased had taken. The liver was very large, weighing seven pounds, and it was in a fairly advanced state of chronic alcoholic inflammation, leading on to what is called gin-drinker's liver – that is the liver which is caused by beer or ardent spirits of any kind. The kidneys were large but healthy. The bladder contained a little fluid and was quite healthy. The other organs in the abdomen were all healthy. Examining the brain I found that it was congested but otherwise perfectly normal. Here, again, I smelled alcohol. I put the stomach and its contents into a jar, sealing and labelling it. The contents of the upper part, three yards or so, of the small intestine I put into another jar, and sealed and labelled that also. These I delivered to Police Constable Valentine on Thursday afternoon. On Friday afternoon, March 1st, considering it possible that more of the fluid might be requisite, I went to the body with Dr. Hampden-Barker, and extracted from the abdominal cavity about 16 oz of the fluid which had escaped from different parts of the body. This also was placed in a jar, and sent for analysis. The cause of death was syncope – that is, failure of the heart, which was not due to disease."

Smelt asked, "Did you suspect any causes?"

"The causes that occurred to me were alcohol, and, either alone or in addition to this, chloroform, chloral, prussic acid, oxalic acid, or some vegetable alkaloid, such as aconitin or atropia. Having heard the evidence I can safely eliminate all but alcohol and chloral, either separate or combined, from the poisons enumerated. The objection to chloral is the absence of smell, which is like that of a freshly-cut cucumber, and not easy to appreciate, and, if present, would have been overshadowed by the strong smell of alcohol. I have known cases occasionally where persons have become rapidly comatose even when apparently not very drunk."

Smelt followed, "If a person were under the influence of drink, and chloral were given him, would it heighten the effect?"

"Certainly."

"Then what might be a safe dose to a sober person would be dangerous to a person under the influence of drink?"

"Yes, because alcohol has the effect of dilating the heart when taken in large doses in a short time, and the administration of chloral under those conditions is dangerous."

"How long does it take for chloral to become absorbed and practically eliminated?"

"Very little absorption would go on after death. In the case of death within a few minutes after administration chloral would be fairly easily discovered. Where death occurs some hours after administration it is more difficult to detect it, and then it would probably be found in the blood. Assuming that a trace of chloral has been discovered in this case, I should say that it would have been likely to hasten death. A dose of 30 grains of chloral has been known to kill an adult. That was with the assistance of alcohol."

Burton, cross-examining, asked Reynolds, "Do you agree with the conclusions of Mr Estcourt and Dr Hampden-Barker?"

Reynolds stated, "I myself did not trace either chloroform or chloral. I agreed with Mr Estcourt generally as to the smells. The deceased had no heart disease. Alcohol was the prevailing smell. My examination led me to the conclusion that the deceased was a man who had led an irregular life, and that he was a drunkard. The brain smelled of alcohol, but that might be produced by drinking a little if death took place within a few minutes after taking the liquor. If a man had disease of the heart the taking of beer, wine or spirits in excess might cause death, but I have cases where I order doses of alcohol with good results to persons suffering from advanced heart disease. The deceased was a very big man and the heart was not unfairly large. The fluid in the stomach smelled of beer. In my opinion beer had been taken shortly before death. I should think the man had had a fair amount of drink before he died. I should think it fairly probable that he was drunk."

Smelt then addressed Caminada, "Is there any evidence about the possession of chloral being traced to Parton?"

Caminada replied "Yes, a Liverpool witness has identified the prisoner as a man who got possession of a bottle of chloral from him on Monday last, but the evidence cannot be produced today."

This led Smelt to conclude that the case would have to be adjourned, but in the meantime evidence could be given as to identification of the prisoner by other witnesses.

PC Jakeman had no doubt that Parton was the man who got into the cab with the deceased at the monument. Cabmen Goulding and Coleman were sure Parton was the person they had both driven.

Caminada then addressed Smelt and stated, "I can bring another witness before you who saw Parton on the dickey with the driver and also saw him get inside the cab."

William Allinson, a detective sergeant, was then called, who said he saw Coleman with his cab standing at the corner of Clarendon Street and Oxford Street. He saw Parton and the driver get off the box. The cabman gave Parton a rug and then he got inside the vehicle. The driver got on the box again and then drove off after the witness had nodded to him. He had no doubt that Parton was the man he saw in the cab. He had seen him before at a boxing contest at the Free Trade Hall.

Smelt then asked Burton, "Would you like Parton to say anything?"

"No, sir; I represent him," replied Burton.

Smelt asked Caminada, "When can you have the other witnesses ready? Can you get them tomorrow?"

"Yes. Parton is before the magistrates in the morning at half-past ten."

Smelt commented, "I suppose a remand will be taken and the proceedings short."

"I understand that will be the case. The whole proceedings will very likely not last more than five or six minutes."

Smelt said, " We have a case fixed for tomorrow morning at nine o'clock in which the same jury are engaged, and we could be ready to resume this inquiry about eleven o'clock."

Caminada asked, "Is it any use bringing Parton here again"?

"No, I don't think so, as he is professionally represented", replied the Deputy Coroner.

Burton commented, "I should like him to be present, as it would assist any cross-examination I might have".

"It is rather hard on the prisoner as we have not the same convenience at the Town Hall for giving him exercise as he would have at the prison", suggested Caminada.

"After that explanation, I will not urge the prisoner's attendance" agreed Burton.

Smelt then inquired of Burton, "Your defence is really an alibi?"

"I would not like to pledge myself to say," replied Burton.

"But an alibi has been set up by the prisoner," responded Smelt.

Burton replied, "I was not instructed until this morning and therefore I would not like to say anything."

"But when the prisoner was before the magistrates he stated, I understand, that he would be able to prove he was elsewhere at the time?"

"He is said to have said that. I don't say what he said, and I would rather not pledge myself to any defence."

At this point Smelt adjourned the inquiry until Tuesday morning at eleven o'clock.

CHAPTER V

The City Police Court, Third Appearance, March 5th

On Tuesday morning, March 5th, Charles Parton was brought before the magistrates for the third time, at the City Police Court. The court was crowded with spectators. The magistrates on the bench were the Stipendiary (Mr Francis J. Headlam) and Mr R. A. Armitage.

Chief Detective Inspector Caminada said, "The prisoner was before the court on Monday and remanded until today. Since he was last before the court, I have made inquiries respecting the robbery on January 8th last from another person, not able to be present today, who has picked out the prisoner from amongst twelve others at the Detective Office in the Town Hall. The man was robbed under similar circumstances to those now being investigated in Fletcher's case, being left helpless and taken into custody by the police. This is an additional case against the Prisoner.

"If the Stipendiary will grant a remand until Thursday, the case will then be complete."

Mr Burton, who again appeared on behalf of the prisoner, said, "I have an application to make. In the medical evidence given yesterday by Mr Estcourt before the Coroner, mention is made of three jars containing parts of this unfortunate man. The contents of the three jars have been subjected to certain analysis, and my application is that the remaining contents of the three jars may be hermetically sealed and kept under the strict surveillance of the police, until the prisoner is committed for trial, as I may hereafter be instructed to make a further application in regard to the jars."

Headlam asked, "Where are they now?"

Caminada replied, "They are in the possession of the City Analyst. They were passed from the Royal Infirmary to the office connected with the Coroner, and from the Coroner to the Analyst."

Headlam added, "It seems to me I have nothing to do with them; they are not in my jurisdiction. I have no doubt they will be carefully kept, and I may say that I think they ought to be properly sealed."

Burton responded, "I will renew my application to the Coroner. I don't make this application in regard to any evidence that has been given. I don't say that any bias has been introduced into the case, but I think, in fairness to the prisoner, that the jars ought to be sealed."

At this point, the case was adjourned until Thursday at 11:30. The prisoner was remanded until Thursday, March 7th and removed from the dock and immediately taken to the Town Hall.

CHAPTER VI

The Coroner's Court, Day Three, March 5th

The Coroner's inquiry into the case of Mr John Fletcher's death resumed at the Courthouse, on the afternoon of Tuesday, March 5th, before Mr Sidney Smelt, Deputy Coroner.

At the outset of the proceedings, Mr William Burton, who again attended on behalf of the prisoner, asked that an order might be issued directing the retention of the jars containing the contents of the stomach and intestines of the deceased gentleman, in order that a fresh analysis might be made if it should seem to the prisoner's relatives desirable. Smelt suggested that Burton should make the application to Mr. Estcourt the city analyst, and said he had no doubt Mr. Estcourt would be only too anxious to further his wishes in every way possible.

Before proceeding with fresh evidence, Smelt sought clarification over the medical evidence. Addressing Dr Ernest Reynolds, who was again in court, he asked, "In your examination yesterday you said that when you made the *post-mortem* examination you found that the blood was extremely fluid, and found no clots. What does that point to you?"

Reynolds replied that, "In cases of chloral poisoning the blood has been found fluid throughout the body. This is not a very common condition. In making *post-mortem* examinations you generally find clots in some parts of the body."

Smelt continued, "That is one of the characteristics of poisoning by chloral?"

Reynolds replied "Yes, sir. The fluidity of the body suggested the presence of chloral"

The first to give fresh evidence was Emily Pearson who proceeded to present the evidence she had previously given at the City Police Court on March 2nd as to seeing Parton in the York Minster on Tuesday evening.

Smelt asked, "Are you quite sure that Parton was the man who was there?"

Pearson replied, "Yes, I am quite sure."

Under cross-examination, Pearson was asked by Burton, "When did you see Parton next?"

She replied, "I next saw Parton on Saturday morning. I carried him in my eye from Tuesday to Friday, and for longer than that. On seeing him at the Town Hall I knew him at once. He was placed with, I think, five other persons, and I at once recognized him."

THE CORONER'S COURT, DAY THREE, MARCH 5TH

Andrew Holt, an old man of eighty-three, said he was step-father to the last witness, who kept house for him at the York Minster beerhouse. Last Tuesday evening he was in the bar-parlour between the hours of seven and eight, and remembered that about 7:10 a young man came in.

Smelt asked, "Was that Charles Parton?"

Holt replied, "To the best of my belief that was the man, but I would not like to swear to him, as this is a matter of life or death, and my memory is not so good now. He ordered some lemonade and gave my daughter two pence for it. While she was out he got up and moved to another part of the room and sat facing me. He seemed put out, almost flabbergasted, by something. When the drink came he asked me if I would take some copper. I said I would take what he had to spare. It then struck me there was something wrong from the way he pulled the money out of his pocket. He pulled out a handful of copper, silver and gold, and placed it on the table, and then picked out two shillings' worth of copper, and my grand daughter gave him a two shilling piece in exchange. Then he asked me if he could have a cab? I said, 'Yes, you will get one at All Saints.' He said he did not know All Saints; he was a stranger in Manchester. 'Oh indeed', I said, 'you are not a native of Manchester?' He said, 'No, I come from London.' He next said, 'I want a cab to drive me to New Cross. Do you know New Cross?' I said, 'Yes,' and then sent for a cab, and gave the man who fetched it the sixpence which the young man had tendered for the service. I told the cabman what he wanted and he had a glass of ginger beer at the expense of the young gentleman. The cabman and the young fellow went out together. Before he got out he stopped close to the cabby and pulled out a watch and asked, 'Is your clock right?' I said, 'Yes,' whereupon he remarked, 'Then it is half-past seven.' The cabby could see the watch at the same time."

Smelt then asked, "Now, have you seen the man since?"

Holt replied, "Last Saturday I went to the Town Hall. They placed eight men before me. I could see which he was, but I would not swear to him."

Smelt continued, "Have you any doubt about the man?"

Holt replied, "I have not the least doubt at all, but on a point of this sort I do not like to swear to him on the grounds of my memory not being as good as it used to be."

The next to give evidence was Frank Spedding of Offerton Mount, Stockport. He said, "I was in the Three Arrows public house, Deansgate, last Tuesday night and saw a man answering the description of the late Mr Fletcher enter in company with a young man, whom I have since identified as Charles Parton. They both seemed sober. Each had a glass of beer, for which the old man paid. They stayed in the room fifteen to twenty minutes, and only took one drink. Whilst in the room they talked together a little and appeared quite friendly. The two men went out, the younger one leading the way. I and the friends with me followed, and I heard the young man say, 'It is on Stretford Road.'"

Smelt asked, "Have you any doubt that Charles Parton is the young man you saw in the Three Arrows?"

"I have no doubt at all," replied Spedding.

Burton asked the witness, "What drew your attention to the pair?"

Spedding replied, "My attention was called to the two men by the fact that there was so little in common between them. They seemed to be such opposite men in character. The deceased was a gentlemanly individual and the other was what I describe as a betting man. That was my opinion of him."

Smelt asked, "When did you next see Parton?"

Spedding replied, "I went to the Town Hall on Saturday and identified Parton as the young man who was with Mr Fletcher."

Burton continued, "Do you remember anything else about that evening?"

Spedding answered, "Yes. When the deceased and Parton entered the Three Arrows a woman, who had been previously making herself obnoxious by talking of three husbands she had buried, went and sat down near the deceased and said, 'This is the sort of man for me.' The deceased simply gave her a look of contempt and did not speak to her. She then went back to her former place and sat down."

The next witness was Charles Bromley, an elderly gentleman who stated, "I am a pharmaceutical chemist and have a shop at No. 1 London Road, Liverpool."

Smelt asked the witness, "Had you anything taken from your shop last week?"

"Yes, a bottle of chloral hydrate," replied Bromley.

Upon being asked by Smelt to give the particulars as to how it was taken, Bromley deposed that, "On Tuesday, February 19th, a person came in about 6:30 in the evening. He said he wanted thirty grains of chloral. I said, 'Where is your prescription?' He replied, 'I have not got a prescription.' I said, 'We never sell chloral without a medical man's prescription. I can't let you have it.' 'Oh, you must oblige me,' he said, 'with ten grains. My mother suffers from *angina pectoris*. You must let me have ten grains. Your assistant knows me.' 'I can't let you have it,' I answered, 'you must show me your doctor's certificate.' 'It is merely word of mouth,' he said, 'do oblige me, for it is a very important thing.' This was repeated several times, and at last I got a fresh bottle containing a pound of chloral and weighed ten grains, but as I was folding up the paper, the young man leaned over the counter, snatched the bottle and ran away. I called loudly after him, but it was of no avail. I gave information to the police the same evening. I have since identified the man as Parton, the prisoner now under remand."

Smelt asked, "Have you any doubt about him?"

"No."

Burton cross-examined the witness to test his recollection of Parton's appearance, but failed to shake his testimony.

Caminada next stated, "That closes the case."

Smelt then stated, "Dr Reynolds has some further evidence to give."

Reynolds was recalled and said, "I had a patient named Parton in one of the medical wards of the Infirmary about six weeks ago. He was suffering from an aneurism, with disease of the heart and *angina pectoris*. I saw him yesterday, and he said that Charles Parton was his son. I cannot remember giving him chloral; it is very probable we should give him morphia or chloral."

Smelt then summed up the case to the jury. "I do not think that after the mass of evidence that has been adduced, that you can hesitate for a moment in coming to a conclusion that a *prima facie* case has been made out that Parton was the man who was with the deceased and that he was the man who went with the deceased to the Three Arrows and to Stretford Road; and if that were so, the only question for your consideration is whether or not he in any way contributed to the death of the deceased by the administration of a drug like chloral. I think you should eliminate everything from your minds but chloral.

"There is no doubt at all that chloral has been traced to Parton's possession and that he knew the properties of chloral; and you only have to consider whether or not a *prima facie* case has been made out that he administered chloral to Mr Fletcher, and so contributed to his death. Now there is no direct evidence on this point. There is no doubt that Mr Fletcher had had a considerable amount of drink – spirits and beer. It was in evidence that he had a glass of beer with Charles Parton at the Three Arrows and Parton would there have had an opportunity of putting a drug like chloral into the beer. The only evidence you have that chloral had been administered was the evidence of Mr Estcourt. Dr Reynolds has told you that chloral is a drug that is rapidly assimilated, and that it is extremely difficult after it has been absorbed by the system to discover it by analysis. He also told you that it would not be surprising if no trace of it were discovered. Mr Estcourt did find a trace of chloral, which is sufficient evidence to satisfy anybody that a *prima facie* case has been made that it had been administered to Mr Fletcher before his death. That is the whole of the evidence as to the presence of chloral in the stomach of the deceased. You have to consider the value of it, and, further, whether there is any strong *prima facie* evidence that chloral had been administered by Parton. The deceased did not show any signs of suffering from the affects of chloral when he left the Three Arrows, and he was with no one but Parton after he left there.

"As to the cause of death, you have been told by Dr Hampden-Barker and Dr Reynolds that the symptoms found after death were consistent with death from alcoholism, which is very similar to succumbing to the affects of chloral. I think it a matter of common surmise, but you also have a strong medical opinion, that a dose of chloral administered to a man under the influence of drink would be extremely likely to cause his death. You have heard all the evidence and it is not necessary that I should go through it. The evidence you have to consider is very small indeed.

"I do not suppose you have any serious doubt but that Parton was with Mr Fletcher, who was under the influence of drink, or that traces of chloral were found in the stomach after death. If the chloral was administered by Parton with the object of committing a robbery and death ensued, that was murder in the eyes of the law. If Parton administered the chloral simply with the object of placing Mr Fletcher under the influence of it, and so caused his death, even then, without any intention of committing a robbery, if Mr Fletcher died, he would be guilty of murder if you think the natural result of administering the chloral would be death. I do not think you could doubt but that the deceased was robbed, and by Parton. Of course I am only speaking of a *prima facie* case being made out. If you have any reasonable doubt as to the possibility of a conviction, you ought not send Parton for trial, but if you think though there is a *prima facie* case, it is your bounden duty to send him for trial on a charge of murder."

The court was then cleared in order that the jury might consider their verdict in private. After consulting together for four or five minutes they announced that they were ready with their verdict.

Smelt addressing the Foreman of the jury asked, "Have you agreed upon your verdict?"

The Foreman replied, "Yes."

"What is your verdict?"

"We are unanimously of the opinion that chloral has been administered to Mr Fletcher, that it has been administered by Charles Parton, and that it has caused his death, and that therefore Parton is guilty of murder."

Smelt then stated, "That is a verdict of wilful murder."

Parton was committed to trial and the witnesses who had not already signed their depositions were then called forward and bound over to give evidence at the Assizes.

The foreman of the jury, addressing Smelt afterwards, stated, "I have been requested by my fellow jurymen to record our sense of the great skill and assiduity displayed by Mr Caminada in the conduct of the case, and we hope Mr Caminada will be recommended for a reward."

Smelt stated that, "I strongly endorse the views of the jury. I consider the manner in which Mr Caminada has investigated and brought before the court the evidence surrounding the death of the late Mr Fletcher reflects very great credit upon him. I think that without any question of reward, the expression of opinion by the jury would, of itself, be fully appreciated by Mr Caminada."

Smelt then closed the proceedings.

CHAPTER VII

The City Police Court, Fourth Appearance, March 7th

On Thursday morning, March 7th, Charles Parton was brought before Mr. Francis Headlam and the magistrates again, at the City Police Court. Mr. William Burton again represented the prisoner and Mr Walter Hocklin appeared in the interest of the relatives of the deceased. On this occasion, Mr William Cobbett appeared to prosecute the case on behalf of the police. Cobbett had been retained to present the police evidence to the magistrates in an effort to have Parton committed to trial.

Cobbett opened the proceedings by stating that he appeared in this case to prosecute on behalf of the Chief Constable. He then summarized the case for the magistrates. "The prisoner, whose name is Charles Parton and who, I believe, is between eighteen and nineteen years of age, seems to have hitherto lived with his parents in Manchester. The charges against him that I intend to proceed with are, first of all, and principally, the charge of murdering Mr Fletcher on the 26th of February – murdering him by administering chloral to him whilst under the influence of liquor. The prisoner will also be charged with the robbery from the person of Mr. Fletcher of a watch and chain and money; the money I think being about £5 in amount, whilst the watch and chain are considered to be of considerable value. The prisoner will also be charged with unlawfully administering a drug to the deceased for the purpose of stupefying him with the intent to commit a felony. There are also other charges against the prisoner, but I do not think it right at present to enter into them or mention them, beyond stating that they exist and will be proceeded with in due course at the close of the principal case.

"The circumstances of the case, taking them in order of date, seem to be these. On February 19th this year, the prisoner was in Liverpool, and about half-past six on the evening of that day he went into the shop of Mr Bromley, chemist, London Road, under the pretence of buying a small quantity of chloral. Whilst Mr Bromley was making it up he stole and ran away with the bottle containing about a pound of chloral. He was not caught and Mr Bromley never heard anything more about him until he was in custody on the present charge. He then identified him and will be called as a witness. My reason for mentioning what took place on February 19th is in order to show that there was a considerable quantity of chloral in the prisoner's possession on that date. The next day of importance is the day on which the alleged murder was committed – Tuesday, February 26th. The deceased, who was a paper manufacturer at Kersley, near Bolton, resided at Southport, and had a place of business or office in Cannon Street, Manchester. He was in Manchester about the middle of the day, and seemed to have left his warehouse or office about one o'clock. A relative of his who was in business with him or was in his employment there took leave of him about a quarter to one, and, at that time, he had the money already mentioned – about £5 – in a purse in one of his pockets and also had the watch and chain. He left his relation with the intention of going to the Mitre Hotel to attend a sale of property there. Subsequently, about a quarter to five in the evening of the same day he was seen by some of the witnesses at the sale at the Mitre Hotel. He seems to have been there until about a quarter or twenty minutes to five, or even past five o'clock, and to have been seen by various persons, who will be called, between four and five, and five and six. At that time he was more or less drunk, but he was still in possession of the watch and showed no sign of being robbed. He was next seen about an hour later in Victoria Street, opposite an oyster shop kept by someone of the name of Sinclair. He was seen there by two or three witnesses and there will not be the slightest doubt that when he was first seen there about a quarter past six o'clock he was in company with the prisoner, standing talking to him in the street. From Victoria Street he went into a cab. A cab was called from the stand which was close to the statue, and he and the prisoner went together to a public house in Deansgate called the Three Arrows. At the Three Arrows they seemed to have remained not a very long time. I have not got the time exactly, and the witnesses do not seem to be able to give it. It seems to have been a quarter of an hour. Whilst there, the deceased had very little to drink. Those who saw him in the public house, and the cabman who saw him enter and come out, did not think he was under the influence of drink. At that time the prisoner was with him, and they were seen with two glasses before them, apparently in quiet conversation, speaking to no one else. When he left the Three Arrows he and the prisoner got into the cab together, and the prisoner gave the cabman instructions to drive to 43, Stretford Road. It will be shown in evidence that No. 43 is a lock-up tailor's shop, only occupied in the daytime whilst the tailors are at their work. In the evening it is locked up, and no one could gain access. It seems to be tolerably evident from what passed between the prisoner and the deceased at the time they entered the cab, that the prisoner represented to the deceased that No. 43, Stretford Road was something different from what it was. The prisoner gave the direction to drive there, and the deceased,

Parton appeared at the City Police Court, Minshull Street on five occasions.

who did not seem, so far as the cabman could judge, to be under the influence of liquor, got into the cab, and the two drove off. The cabman will tell his Worship the circumstances of the drive and the streets he drove along.

"The next matter that is of importance took place when they got to Cavendish Street. There some passer-by called the cabman's attention to the fact that the cab door was open and that one of his passengers, or passenger as the passer-by thought, had got out and ran away. That caused the cabman to stop. Some other person came up to the cab, and the deceased was found to be still inside. He was lying with his head on the front seat while he was sitting on the back one, so he was in a sort of stooping position resting his forehead on the front seat. He appeared to be in a state of semi-stupor. He could not speak, and he resisted some efforts made to rouse him up. That was the condition he was found in. The cabman, after endeavouring to rouse him, shut the door and drove the cab back to the stand from which he had come, in Victoria Street. He came across a constable who was on the beat there of the name of Jakeman, and called his attention to the state of the deceased. He told him all the facts so far as he knew them, and the constable told him to drive him to the Infirmary. He got inside the vehicle for the purpose of accompanying the cabman to that institution, and on the way there the constable seemed to have found that the deceased was in a very bad if not dying state, and actually died as they were carrying him from the cab to the Infirmary. The constable also said that when he got into the cab there were signs that the deceased had been robbed. His watch and chain were gone, and the lower part of his waistcoat seemed to have been lifted up in a hurried way, as if someone had been trying to get at the trouser pockets.

"Returning to the disappearance of the prisoner, he is reported to have left the cab about seven o'clock in Cavendish Street. About ten or fifteen minutes past seven o'clock he entered a public house in Higher Chatham Street, and there had something to drink. In the course of the conversation he produced a watch, which from the general description given by those who saw it, resembled in a great degree the watch which belonged to Mr Fletcher. The prisoner also seemed to have a pocket full of money, as he showed a considerable amount and obtained some change. Ultimately, about twenty minutes past seven, a cab was sent for, the prisoner got inside, and he was driven to the Locomotive Inn, in Oldham Road. He was then lost sight of, and nothing further was seen of him until he was taken into custody.

"When the deceased was taken into the Infirmary and he was discovered to be dead, an external examination was made for the purpose of ascertaining the cause of death, but of course, no *post-mortem* examination was made that night. The next day, however, a *post-mortem* examination was made and it was found that Mr Fletcher had died from syncope, and that syncope was not due to disease. The deceased, as a matter of fact, appears to have been a healthy man, and the doctor was satisfied beyond all question that the syncope was not due to disease. Syncope might be produced either by alcohol or chloral, if either was taken in an excessive amount and might be produced still more easily by both combined. The effect of either produces dilation of the heart and dilation produces syncope. The contents of the deceased's stomach and intestines were almost immediately, after the *post-mortem* examination, submitted to Mr Estcourt, the city analyst, for examination, and he discovered on analysis that there were traces of chloral. There was no difficulty in discovering traces of alcohol and in the opinion of the medical men engaged in the case, there was no doubt that Mr Fletcher died from the effects of chloral and alcohol combined.

"So far as I am aware, the prisoner and Mr Fletcher were unacquainted before the night in question and how they came to enter into conversation in Victoria Street remains unexplained. Bearing in mind the fact that on February 19th, the prisoner got possession of a large quantity of chloral, and also the fact that during the time the prisoner was in company with Mr Fletcher, no one else was with them, and that Mr Fletcher's watch chain and purse disappeared, the inference is that the prisoner administered the chloral, and he left the deceased in a state of stupefaction. Assuming these facts are true, I think the Bench will be compelled to send this most serious case for investigation elsewhere."

A number of witnesses who were previously examined at the inquest before the Deputy City Coroner were then called. They corroborated Cobbett's opening statement as to the identity of Fletcher and the prisoner and their movements on the day in question. The case was then adjourned until Friday, for the medical evidence to be examined.

CHAPTER VIII

The City Police Court, Fifth Appearance, March 8th

The City Police Court hearing resumed, on the morning of Friday, March 8th. At the time fixed for the resumption of proceedings there seemed to be no perceptible diminution of the interest taken in the case, as the court was crowded in every part.

The medical evidence was initially gone into. Dr John Hampden-Barker, late house surgeon at the Royal Infirmary, and Dr Ernest Reynolds, resident medical officer at the Royal Infirmary, repeated the evidence they had given before the Deputy Coroner on March 4th.

Under cross-examination Reynolds was asked to describe the condition of the deceased's liver. In reply to Burton, the witness said, "I do not consider, despite its abnormal size, that Mr Fletcher had a typical 'gin-drinker's' liver. In my opinion, assuming that the deceased was drunk, death was due to a dose of chloral having been administered to him whilst he was in that condition."

Burton continued, "Dr Reynolds, what is chloral used for?"

"I have used it for the last six years. It is a very common drug used for neuralgia and other ailments."

"Other ailments such as insomnia?"

"Yes."

"If the deceased was in the habit of taking chloral to help him sleep, would this effect his health?"

"In my opinion, if a man troubled with insomnia had been in the habit of taking chloral for a period of two or three months, it might have had a deleterious effect upon his health."

At this point Headlam interjected, "I do not see the object of all this."

Burton replied, "To show that death arose from natural causes; that the deceased contributed to his own death."

Headlam continued, "You had the deceased's nephew in the box, and you never asked him a word about this."

"I asked him about his general health and he said that his uncle had been ailing for some time. He had gone thinner in the last fifteen months."

Burton than asked the witness, "If the deceased had been in the habit of taking chloral hydrate, and had been a drinking man, would that have had any affect upon his health? Would it have contributed to cause death?"

Reynolds replied, "It might have done. I would not like to say that a man who has been in the habit of taking chloral hydrate would be more likely to die than a man who has not."

Mr Charles Estcourt, City Analyst, then said he had submitted the contents of the jars sent to him for analysis to a very delicate chemical test, and in two of them he found traces of chloroform, the result of decomposition of chloral hydrate.

At this point Cobbett stated, "That closes this case."

Burton then stated, "At the present time, as I am instructed, there will be a complete answer to all the charges against the prisoner."

The Court was then adjourned until two o'clock.

Upon resumption, Cobbett said, "I now propose to charge the prisoner with having robbed John Parkey, a porter in the employ of the M. S. and L. Railway Company at the Ashton, Oldham Road station upon December 28th. He will also be charged with administering a drug to the man with the intent to commit a felony."

Parkey and Coxon went to the Old Wheat Sheaf prior to bumping into the Parton brothers.

John Parkey, porter, residing at 32, Uxbridge Street, Ashton-under-Lyne then gave evidence. "I came to Manchester on December 28th, last year. When I arrived in Manchester I accidentally met a friend named Thomas Coxon and we went to the market to look after some poultry. Afterwards we went to the Old Wheat Sheaf in High Street, stayed half an hour, had three glasses of beer there, and left about a quarter past nine o'clock for London Road station. We walked down High Street, to Market Street and into Piccadilly. As we were passing the White Bear Inn in Piccadilly, Coxon met the prisoner and his brother. I was introduced to them and we all went into the White Bear around twenty minutes past nine and I paid for a round of drinks. We all left at a quarter to ten o'clock and proceeded

Parkey went to the White Bear Inn with Coxon and the Parton brothers.

along Piccadilly until we arrived at Port Street and, at the solicitation of Parton, we went into the Crown and Anchor. We had another beer there, making five in total, and we all sat around one table with me and Parton at one side and Coxon and the prisoner's brother at the other side. All I remember after that was seeing the barman bringing in the beer we had ordered. I did not come to myself until four o'clock the following morning, when I found myself lying on the floor of my friend Coxon's bedroom. I was missing my silver lever watch and chain and 18s. 6d. in money. When I came to myself, my inside was very much upset and I was frothing at the mouth. These ill effects continued for five days afterwards, and I was unable to eat any food during that time, as any attempt to do so made me sick. I have not felt perfectly well since."

Headlam asked, "When did you report what happened to the police?"

Parkey responded, "The day after the incident, on December 29th."

Under cross-examination by Burton, Parkey was asked, "Were you drunk? Were you in Manchester on a drinking spree? Did you not see anything suspicious?"

The witness responded, "I never had anything to drink until we went to the Old Wheat Sheaf Hotel. I was not on a drunken spree. I only had five beers in all. I do not remember leaving the Crown and Anchor or being in a cab and remember nothing till four o'clock the next morning when I awoke and missed my watch. I was very sick the next morning, although Coxon was not. I am not quite right yet."

"Did you at any time go outside with a woman?"

"I do not remember that I ever left the room after I got to the Crown and Anchor. I have no recollection of doing so and at no time after I met the prisoner was I in company with a woman. I never saw a woman, at all. I believe the prisoner stole my watch in the Crown and Anchor."

Thomas Coxon, clerk, lodging at 22, Higher Chatham Street, said, "I met John Parkey on December 28th about a quarter past seven in the evening and we went to the Old Wheat Sheaf together. We left there together about a quarter past nine. I knew the time because Parkey looked at his watch, but this was the last occasion on which I saw his watch. As we past the White Bear Inn we saw the prisoner and his brother standing close to the door. I have known the elder one for five or six years, but I have only known the younger for about six months. We all went in, stayed a short time and left walking along Piccadilly. At the invitation of the elder Parton we all went up Port Street to the Crown and Anchor at the corner with Hilton Street. We ordered glasses of beer and during the course of a conversation about boxing the prisoner and Parkey had a few high words, but apparently they became reconciled. At this point the elder brother asked me to come to the door as he had something to say to me. On reaching the door the elder Parton then said that Parkey and the prisoner would make it up themselves and asked me to come out and have a drink. I, not thinking anything was wrong, went with him to another public house close by. Before I left the Crown and Anchor I saw Parkey drink the beer that had been brought in. At the time I left there was only the prisoner and Parkey in the room. I was away for about ten minutes, and on my return to the Crown and Anchor I found a cab at the front door, and the barman and the prisoner hauling and pulling Parkey about to get him out of the public house, into the street and into the cab. He was not able to stand or walk. I asked the prisoner what happened, as I had left him alright. The prisoner replied that he thought Parkey had been round the corner with some woman and must have been drugged. At first one of the Partons suggested that Parkey should be taken to their house, but I negatived that, and finally had him taken to my lodgings in the cab. Despite all my efforts and the people at my lodgings, Parkey remained insensible until four o'clock the following morning. In my opinion Parkey looked like a man who had been stupefied."

Coxon, under cross examination by Burton, was asked, "How do you know the prisoner's brother?"

Coxon replied, "The prisoner's brother works in the wholesale fish and game market, where I myself also work. I have worked in the market for five or six years and the prisoner's brother has worked there about as long."

Burton continued, "Tell me about the disagreement?"

"There were some words or wrangling in the Crown and Anchor about the prisoner's boxing. The prisoner's brother said that the prisoner and Parkey will make it up presently and suggested we go and have a drink round the corner. The next day the prisoner and his brother came and called at my stall and asked how my friend was and how he had gone on. I said he was nearly dead, that I thought he had been drugged and that something had been done to him; that there had been some foul play."

"Did you accuse either of the brothers of stealing your friend's watch?"

"No, I did not think it my place to do so. My friend went to the detective office about the case."

"Did it never strike you that the prisoner had stolen your friend's watch – not when you saw this 'cab mystery' in the papers?"

"It struck me he must have met with some foul play in that house."

Alfred Moxon, barman at the Crown and Anchor, Port Street, was the next witness called. He stated, "I remember four men coming to our house a few days after Christmas, shortly after ten o'clock in the evening." He could identify Coxon and Parkey, but he could not speak to the other two men. Moxon served them with four glasses of beer. "All the men seemed to be perfectly sober. Two of the party went out of the house first; one of them was Coxon. After the two had gone out Parkey went to the lavatory in the yard, leaving the other man alone in the room. He seemed alright as he came back from the lavatory. I had my attention called to Parkey a few minutes afterwards and he was quite stupefied. Upon seeing that, I asked the other man in the room what had happened as Parkey was alright not a half minute ago. The other man did not know what the matter

THE CITY POLICE COURT, FIFTH APPEARANCE, MARCH 8TH

with him was. A cab was fetched and just as we were getting Parkey into it, Coxon returned."

In reply to cross-examination by Burton asking if he suspected foul play, Moxon said, "I never had an idea that there had been foul play."

Reynolds when questioned stated, "I have heard the evidence given in the case, and in my opinion the description of the stupefaction of Parkey and subsequent recovery, are entirely consistent with the symptoms of chloral having been administered to him. The state of coma was too sudden to be due to alcohol."

Cobbett then said, "The prisoner will now be charged with yet another offence of the kind alleged against him with regard to Parkey. He will be charged with having on January 8th in the present year stolen from the person of Samuel Oldfield a watch and chain, and some money, and he will also be charged, in the same way as before, with administering a drug to him for the purpose of stupefying him and committing a felony. The circumstances of this case are not unlike the last."

Samuel Oldfield, grocer, 95 Welbeck Street, Ashton-under-Lyne, was then called. He said, "On January 8th, I was in Manchester, having been in the city during the day for the purpose of transacting some business. Around nine that night I was in the Slip Inn, Blue Boar Court. I had had some drink, but was quite sober. When I had been in the house a little while, I saw the prisoner come in. We had drinks together and then went to the Blue Boar Hotel, just around the corner from the Slip Inn, and entered a room on the ground floor. The room was empty when we went in. Directly after we arrived, the prisoner handed me a glass, said it was for me and asked me to drink it. After I had drunk it I remarked to the prisoner that he had not put much water in it as it was stronger than I had been drinking before. We next had some drink at the bar, which also tasted stronger than I had been drinking. The drink was handed to me in each case by the prisoner. We left the house at eleven o'clock, and when we emerged into the street I became unconscious. I remember coming to my senses at daylight in a police cell. I was brought up at the City Police Court the next morning and fined 5s. for being drunk. At the time I became insensible I had upon me a silver watch, a gold chain and about £4 in money."

Parton took Oldfield to the Blue Boar Hotel to complete his drugging and robbery.

Under cross-examination, Burton asked, "Were you drunk when you got to the second public house?"

Oldfield replied, "Although I had had some drink during the day, I was not drunk when I got to the Blue Boar Hotel. At first I did not think I had been drugged. It was only when I read of these proceedings in the papers that I came to the conclusion that I, too, had been drugged."

Jessie Mutten, barman at the Blue Boar Hotel, spoke to seeing the prisoner and Oldfield together in the house on the night in question. "When they went out together they both seemed to be sober."

Thomas Robinson, cabdriver, 9, Turner Street, Rusholme, said, "On January 8th, I was driving along Corporation Street past the corner of Todd Street about a quarter past eleven, when I was hailed by a young man whom I believe to be the prisoner, who told me to come down Todd Street to a warehouse door, in which, upon the steps, I found Oldfield lying and unable to speak. I helped the young man to place Oldfield in the cab and then he told me to drive down Oldham Road to the Cheshire Cheese public house. As I was driving along Oldham Road, a woman in the street called to me. She noticed the cab door was open and saw somebody get out of it. I got down and examined my cab and found that the young man had gone, having escaped from the cab whilst it was in motion. Oldfield was in the same position as before. I took him to Goulden Street police station. The officer on duty there judged that the man was not suffering from the effects of drink entirely, and believing that something else was the matter and that he should have medical assistance, told me to take him and Oldfield to the Royal Infirmary."

William Doughty, police constable, corroborated the evidence of the last witness as to seeing Oldfield in his cab at the police station. "When I found him his right hand trouser pocket was turned inside out. The only money he had upon him was sixpence. He was taken to the Infirmary and was treated by Dr Thomas Goodfellow, who at first thought he was suffering from opium poisoning from the look in his eyes. A stomach pump was used and various restoratives were applied. Afterwards he thought he was simply suffering from the effects of alcohol. As soon as he was brought to, he became aware that he had lost his watch, chain and money."

Cobbett concluded by saying, "That completes the case for the prosecution."

Burton said that, "On behalf of the prisoner, I might say that he has a complete answer to all the charges made against him, and that at the proper time that defence will be put in."

The prisoner was then committed to take his trial at the ensuing Liverpool Assizes on all the charges preferred against him.

PART TWO
THE POLICE INVESTIGATION

CHAPTER IX

The Police Investigation, February 27th

On the morning of Wednesday, February 27th, 1889, Jerome Caminada was brought in by the Chief Constable of Manchester to lead the investigation in determining whether the mysterious death of John Fletcher was due to natural causes or if something more sinister had taken place. Caminada was Chief Detective Inspector in the detectives division of the Manchester police force at the time.

The inquest into the death of John Fletcher had been set for Friday, March 1st before the Deputy Coroner. Caminada began his investigation by studying intently the slim file of reports on the case in his office, and reading the facts so far established, including the statements made by cabman Harry Goulding and police constable William Jakeman. He read that when the body of the deceased was examined at the Infirmary by Dr John Hampden-Barker on the evening of February 26th, he could find no signs of violence and no tell-tale signs that death had been induced by poisoning. Indeed, he reported to PC Jakeman, "As far as I can see he took a drink too many. After all, that's all it takes, just the one."

The medical report of Dr Hampden-Parker, coupled with the statements made by PC Jakeman and the cab driver, seemed to settle the matter. It was simply a case of two companions out drinking for the day and the older one's heart having given out as a result of excessive drinking. It was supposed that the younger of the two, observing his companion's

Manchester Town Hall. Caminada had his office in the basement of Manchester Town Hall.

deteriorating condition, panicked and jumped out of the moving cab. His motive was nothing more than not to get involved in any official inquiry.

However, examination of the clothing of the deceased by Jakeman at the Infirmary revealed that there was no money whatever in any of the pockets. A cheque book issued by the Southport branch of the Manchester and Salford Bank was all that was found.

Caminada's first priority was to identify the deceased. He decided to dispatch his deputy, Inspector Samuel Wilson, to the Manchester and Salford bank in Mosley

Street with the cheque book and a description of the deceased in hand. The manager was able to inform Wilson that the account number on the cheques corresponded to that of an account held at the Southport branch in the name of John Fletcher, an important and well known customer of the bank. The manager added that John Fletcher's company, Messrs. Robert Fletcher and Son of Cannon Street in Manchester, held an account at his branch in the city. The manager also confirmed that the description of the deceased matched that of John Fletcher.

Wilson next proceeded to Cannon Street and at the premises of Messrs. Robert Fletcher and Son, met a Robert Fletcher. Fletcher was about to leave to meet his uncle, John Fletcher, at the company mill in Stoneclough. He recognized the description of the deceased and identified the cheque book as belonging to his uncle. Robert Fletcher had last seen his uncle the day before at his place of business. He left to attend the sale of a mill at the Mitre Hotel. When asked if he knew whether the deceased was planning on meeting anybody at the auction, Robert Fletcher replied that his uncle had indicated that he expected to come across George Wild and William Hall there, two business associates of his. Robert Fletcher was able to supply the Inspector with both their business addresses in the centre of the city. Wilson then, accompanied by Robert Fletcher, returned to the Detective Office where they met with the Chief Detective Inspector. The three proceeded to the Infirmary where Robert Fletcher identified the deceased as his uncle.

Upon returning to the detective office, Caminada further questioned Robert Fletcher and ascertained that John Fletcher was a gentleman well known on the Exchange, the senior partner in the aforementioned paper manufacturer with offices in the city, a justice of the peace, and a member of the Lancashire County Council. He was a widower and had made his fortune from the paper business. He left his home, some distance from Manchester, on the morning of February 26th, taking with him some under-linen and other articles, as he purposed to stay at Knutsford until the week-end. On his arrival in Manchester he proceeded to the offices of his firm and when he left he was wearing a watch and chain worth about one hundred and twenty pounds. He told his nephew upon leaving, "I will meet you at the mill tomorrow morning."

Having put Robert Fletcher in a cab to take him back to his Cannon Street office, the Chief Detective Inspector and Wilson discussed the case and decided on their next steps. Wilson was to interview George Wild and William Hall while Caminada was to pay a visit to the address 43, Stretford Road, mentioned in Goulding's statement.

Wilson first went to George Wild's business address and then to the offices of William Hall. Both confirmed seeing Fletcher at the Mitre Hotel on the 26th.

Meanwhile, The Chief Detective Inspector took a cab to 43, Stretford Road. The address was a shop occupied by a tailoring business. Harry Smith, who was employed there, stated that his employer never had any dealings with a Mr Fletcher, nor with a person meeting the description of his young companion, and he could suggest no reason as to why they should wish to visit their shop. Caminada asked Smith if he was willing to go to the Infirmary. He agreed and the Chief Detective Inspector escorted him there. Smith was unable to recognize the body of John Fletcher, which confirmed his statement that John Fletcher was not known to him or his company.

Next, Caminada took his cab to the Three Arrows, also mentioned in Goulding's statement. Mary Ross, landlady, said that Fletcher, accompanied by a young man, came into the hotel about half-past six o'clock on Tuesday evening. She served them with drink in the smokeroom. Fletcher ordered the drinks – two bitter beers. She served him, and he paid for them. He tendered a shilling, and that was all the money she saw he had. Fletcher drank the beer during the time she was getting change. The men only had one drink each and did not seem to talk much to each other. She did not know the young man and could only give a vague description.

Caminada, having reviewed the statements of Wild and Hall, next decided to visit Sinclair's oyster rooms, mentioned by Hall as Fletcher's destination upon leaving the Mitre Hotel, to determine if Fletcher went there on Tuesday evening. Nobody remembered seeing such a gentleman, alone or with a young companion. However, outside Sinclair's, at 10 Victoria Street, was a stall for the sale of dried fish and game. Caminada approached the stall and the proprietor, Edward Lait, knew Fletcher well and often saw him in Victoria Street near his stall. He confirmed having seen Fletcher on Tuesday evening standing in the street close to his stall at about 6:40 in the company of a young man. Shortly before, he had seen Fletcher alone coming through the Shambles from the direction of Kenyon's (the Wellington Inn) public house in Market Place. Lait did not notice when Fletcher left, who he thought was very much the worse for drink.

CHAPTER X

The Police Investigation, February 28th

The next morning, Caminada took time to reflect on the case. The Coroner's Court had scheduled the inquest for the following day and Caminada needed to be fully prepared. He contacted the Coroner's Office and instructed warrants to be issued for his key witnesses to appear at the inquest: Robert Fletcher (nephew of the deceased), George Wild and William Hall (business associates of the deceased), Edward Lait and Harry Smith (shop keepers), and Harry Goulding (cabman).

In the course of his early inquiries Caminada had learned that when he left his firm's offices, the deceased was wearing a watch and chain worth about one hundred and twenty pounds, and was also in possession of a purse containing gold, from which he took a sovereign at the Mitre Hotel. Upon his clothes being searched strong presumptive evidence was afforded that the deceased had been robbed, since no money or valuables of any kind were found upon him. In addition, when leaving the Three Arrows, Fletcher's young companion told the cabman to go to an address that was obviously a blind; one chosen at random, presumably to take them away from the busy city centre and give the young man time to act.

It no longer appeared to be a case of a heart giving out, induced by alcohol, and a young companion panicking and fleeing the scene. Caminada was convinced that a robbery had been perpetrated but

Fletcher and Parton went to the Three Arrows (right) after leaving the Cathedral.

he was also beginning to suspect that poisoning may have been involved. Consequently, the Chief Detective Inspector sent a note to Sidney Smelt, the Deputy Coroner, alerting him to his suspicions. Smelt subsequently instructed the medical men at the Infirmary and the city analyst to pay particular attention to any evidence of poisoning during the *post-mortem* examination. Whether a more serious crime had been committed could not be cleared up until the result of the *post-mortem* examination was made known; but the result of his inquiries justified Caminada in searching for the unknown young man, and asking for some explanation of his mysterious conduct.

Who was the youth? All Caminada had were conflicting eye witness descriptions. He was someone about five feet two inches or five feet three inches in height, clean shaven, with a fresh complexion, wearing a brown or light check suit and a felt hat; or, as another account put it, about five feet four inches in height, with a light complexion, and rather red faced. "Certainly, there were few clues to work on."

In order to find the youth, a thorough knowledge of the city and how and where to elicit information would be essential. Caminada thought to himself, "The old Market Place is the rendezvous of all kinds and conditions of men. Here can be found the cotton merchants, the bookmarker, the blackleg, the broken-down clerk or warehouseman, the man who lives by his wits, and the man who has no wits but dodgery to live upon. Here it was, without doubt, that the deceased paper merchant with his money had dropped across his young companion, who was evidently using his wits for his living." According to William Hall, Fletcher had left the Mitre Hotel about half-past five, and the two had been seen together near the Market Place about an hour later by Edward Lait. The Chief Detective Inspector was also certain that, "Here, in the Market Place, he should probably hear something of the young culprit who was wanted, for probably he was one of the many who frequent the place like sparrow-hawks to prey upon their victims."

Adopting a number of disguises, Caminada spent many hours in the afternoon and evening of Thursday, February 28th, leaning on grubby bar counters talking to numerous people, including known criminals. He reported, "I back chatted with hard-faced women. I picked up scraps of information like a bird picks up scraps of bread. Some scraps were tall tales, some outrageous lies, but a few had a flavour of truth." Nevertheless, his inquiries proved futile; many had seen them together, but no one could give him any information respecting the young fellow. The people who had seen them together included Frank Spedding who the Chief Detective Inspector came across in the Wellington Inn. Spedding was in the Three Arrows on Tuesday night and had heard Parton say, "Its on Stretford Road" as he was leaving with Fletcher.

No one though, could give the Chief Detective Inspector any information respecting the identity of the young man. However, quite fortuitously, Caminada picked up a lead to the working man who had seen Fletcher's companion jump from the cab in Stretford Road. He questioned a man, David Watts, at Sinclair's oyster rooms. Watts told him that last night he fell into conversation with a young warehouseman. The warehouseman told him of his experience on the night of February 26th. He could not recall the warehouseman's name, but did remember that he worked at the Great Northern Railway Company's Goods Warehouse in Watson Street.

THE POLICE INVESTIGATION, FEBRUARY 28TH

The Chief Detective Inspector proceeded to Watson Street and met with the foreman. The warehouseman had related the story to his workmates and so Caminada was soon talking to John Needham. Needham informed him that about 7:30 pm last Tuesday he was in Stretford Road, near Lipton's provision shop, and saw a cab driving towards Stretford. Just after the vehicle had passed him he saw a man put his hand out of the near side window, open the door, and disembarked as the cab was going. After reaching the footpath the man turned back towards All Saints' church. Needham smiled at the occurrence and thinking the man was cheating the cabman and that it was no business of his to interfere, allowed the man to pass. He afterwards saw the cab had stopped at the corner of Renshaw Street, and he went to it and saw Goulding examining Fletcher. He assisted in attempts to arouse the old gentleman and noticed that he was not wearing a gold watch and chain. Needham thought the deceased was in a very bad condition from drink. The cabman then drove on and again stopped at Boundary Street, where they again tried to rouse the deceased. They failed and the cabman then said he would drive to where the policeman had seen him pick up his fare and Needham went on his way. Needham did not know the man who alighted from the cab and could only give Caminada a vague description, but thought he would be able to recognize the man again.

The only fresh information gathered from this was the direction which the companion of the deceased had taken after he had jumped from the cab; back along Cavendish Street towards All Saint's church at the corner with Oxford Street.

CHAPTER XI

The Police Investigation, March 1st

Early morning, March 1st, saw the Chief Detective Inspector in his office preparing to give evidence at the Coroner's Court. Early in the afternoon, following his appearance there, he was called into the Chief Constable's office to present an update on progress in the case. Caminada told the Chief Constable that it no longer seemed to be a case of accidental death from drinking too much alcohol – he now suspected that the deceased had been induced to drink poison to aid in a robbery which resulted in the death of Fletcher.

This investigation was being conducted in the shadow of the Whitechapel murders. Between August 31st and November 9th, 1888, "Jack the Ripper" was responsible for the brutal murder of five women prostitutes in that poor district of London. It was now only four months after these murders and the identity of the perpetrator remained unknown. This resulted in much pressure on police forces nation wide to rapidly solve crime, particularly those of a violent nature and involving murder.

The Chief Constable's response to the Chief Detective Inspector's update was, "So it looks like murder with a motive – robbery," and demanded, "find the young man he was travelling with and bring him in for questioning." The pressure was now really on Caminada to arrest the youth. John Needham had reported that the young companion had fled in the direction of All Saint's church upon jumping from the cab.

43 Stretford Road was the destination for Fletcher and Parton's cab ride.

Late Friday afternoon, the Chief Detective Inspector decided to start where the young man had been seen alighting from the cab and he proceeded along Stretford Road and then Cavendish Street in the direction of All Saint's. As he walked, he talked to people on the street and visited pubs and shops he passed, describing the man he was looking for. He was, "banking, or betting, that a man flush with gold sovereigns and sporting an extremely expensive watch could not help but be noticed and remembered." At the corner of Cavendish Street and Chatham Street he looked to the left and to the right. He noticed a public house to the right along Higher Chatham Street. He proceeded down this street and at the corner with Boundary Street, he entered a public house called the Salutation Tavern. However, nobody in the pub could help. He then continued along Higher Chatham Street and at the corner with Booth Street, entered another pub called the York Minster. Emily Pearson, house keeper to her father and landlord, Andrew Holt, stated that a young man somewhat answering the description given had paid a visit to their beerhouse last Tuesday night. She then gave Caminada the information she would later depose at the City Police Court on March 2nd. Pearson then got her father who relayed to Caminada the evidence he would give at the Coroner's Court on March 5th.

Caminada asked the landlord if he knew the cabbie or knew what the young man's destination was. Neither he nor his daughter could help – the cabbie was a total stranger but Andrew Holt remembered the young man negotiating a fare to New Cross. Coincidentally, in the bar at the time the Chief Detective Inspector was making his inquiries was a Thomas Hibbs. Hibbs stated that he was in the bar on February 26th and he was the person who actually went to get a cab for the youth and received 6d. for his trouble. He could not help with the identification of the cabman but had definitely heard the destination of the young man as "New Cross." Neither Holt nor Hibbs heard his specific destination at New Cross.

Feeling sure he was on the right track, Caminada was anxious to find where in New Cross the young man was taken. He went straight to the cab stand at the Cathedral steps in search of the cabman who had taken the youth away from the public house. There he found Harry Goulding, the cabman who had driven Fletcher and Parton to Stretford Road, waiting for a fare. The Chief Detective Inspector asked his assistance in finding the cabman who drove the young man from the York Minster to New Cross. Goulding said he would make inquiries with his fellow cabbies and let him know what he found. Caminada returned to the Town Hall and about two hours later there was a knock at his office door. Harry Goulding entered and stated, "I have found your cabman." Goulding had spent the last couple of hours driving round the city centre talking to various cabmen. He found William Coleman on his cab at the All Saint's cab stand in Oxford Street. Coleman confirmed he took a fare from the York Minster on Tuesday evening. "He's agreed to meet you in the 'Hidden Gem' at four o'clock this afternoon to tell you what he knows". Caminada thanked Goulding, gave him a florin (2s.) for his trouble and left to meet Coleman. At the appointed time, Caminada met Coleman and the latter stated that he took the young man to the Locomotive Inn, Oldham Road, New Cross and also spoke to a police sergeant whom he knew, Detective Sergeant Allinson, while on route.

Proceeding to the Locomotive Inn, the Chief Detective Inspector was baffled, for the staff knew nothing whatever of a young man arriving there on the night of February 26th. It was a busy place, though, and Caminada supposed that the customer might have gone unnoticed. Even so, the Chief Detective Inspector believed his suspect was, "a show-off; a man who spent freely, flaunted his stolen watch and chain, called for cabs, and so on, all aimed at getting him envious glances." This behaviour will help me track him down," thought Caminada.

The Chief Detective Inspector now took time to consider the evidence compiled so far. It appeared that his visit to the Locomotive Inn pointed to the young man being connected in some way or other with the pugilistic fraternity. Caminada knew the pub well, a place known to locals as, "Jack Rooks," and a notorious haunt for boxers, their managers and the touts who hung on the fringes of the boxing sporting world. The investigation seemed to be on the right track – a drug called chloral hydrate was well known in criminal circles for its powerful effect in "knock-out drops." Poisoning of John Fletcher with chloral hydrate was consistent with the evidence surrounding his death.

He next started to make a list of the various questionable characters who had at different times made the Locomotive Inn their port of call. In addition, he interviewed, "A motley crew with flat noses and cauliflower ears to find if they knew anything about the crime." High on Caminada's list was a man known as "Pig Jack" Parton who had a police record and lived in Cornwall Street, Oldham Road, close by the Locomotive Inn. Upon reviewing "Pig Jack's" record the Chief Detective Inspector was able to ascertain that "Pig Jack" had once kept a pub in Greengate, Salford. In his youth "Pig Jack" had been a professional light-heavyweight boxer of some repute. When he retired from the ring he became a small time promoter and used his pub as the venue for fights he promoted. He was known to make very large bets on the contests he arranged, and rumour had it that "Pig Jack" had found it profitable to drug the mouth wash provided for the opponents of his own fighters. Observing how well this worked, "Pig Jack" raised his villainy to a new level. He would drug the patrons of his pub by adding knock-out drops to their beer. "Pig Jack's" customers gradually fell off. Many complained to the police, tired of waking up in back alleys with their pockets empty, and "Pig Jack" lost his pub license. This further intensified Caminada's belief that chloral was involved, and he immediately sent a message to the Deputy Coroner so that the medical men could be instructed to look specifically for evidence of poisoning by chloral hydrate.

"Pig Jack" seemed a prime suspect. However, by now he was too old and feeble to be considered a suspect. He could never be mistaken for an eighteen-year old youth. However, "Pig Jack's" son was a different matter. Charles Parton was exactly eighteen years old and a younger edition of his father. Caminada thought it perfectly reasonable to assume that Charles had learned his knowledge of chloral from his father, "What is more likely than that the son had learned this drugging propensity at home? The more I thought of the matter, the more I felt convinced that I was on the right track, and at length I determined to arrest him."

Assuming the Partons would pay a visit to their local that evening with their newly found wealth, the Chief Detective Inspector kept watch at the Inn until he saw Charles enter with his father. Caminada was concerned, though – Charles wasn't wearing the watch and was several inches taller than 5 ft. 3 in. and also had a moustache. However, the Chief Detective Inspector reasoned that since the cabbies were looking down on their passengers from the driver's seat, they might underestimate the height of their fares. The moustache was clearly a new facial feature less than a week old. They both left the bar an hour later in company with two other individuals discussing where they intended to go for their next drink.

Upon leaving the Locomotive Inn, Charles Parton briefly exchanged a few words with a man who was just entering the establishment. Once the two Partons were out of sight, Caminada entered the public house and approached the man who was now standing at the bar. Thomas Eastwood was well acquainted with Charles Parton. Indeed, Eastwood saw Parton getting into a cab at the Cathedral steps on Tuesday evening. He was also able to tell Caminada that Parton was living with his parents in Cornwall Street.

CHAPTER XII

The Police Investigation, March 2nd

Convinced he had found his man, the Chief Detective Inspector went to the Chief Constable to announce that he was ready to make an arrest. He further added that he needed help because he thought Charles Parton's father might intervene with his fists. Caminada was given two other detectives, Detective Sergeants Harris and Schofield, and with Inspector Wilson went to Cornwall Street. "Going thither they found that they were too late; the birds had flown two days before." At the address the windows were curtainless and no one answered the door. It was a neighbour who inquired if they were looking for "Pig Jack?"

"Is he about?" Caminada asked.

The neighbour responded, "He's gone,

The Cheshire Cheese was Parton's destination after leaving the York Minister.

they've all gone, those Partons and good riddance. Don't ask me where. I suggest you ask at the pub." So saying, the neighbour pointed to the Cheshire Cheese Tavern, at the corner of Cornwall Street and Oldham Road. There, a nervous barman suggested they inquire at 12, Moore Street, Rochdale Road. Proceeding to this address, the Chief Detective Inspector decided to watch the house for a while and to his delight, saw "Pig Jack" leave the house alone. Immediately, at half-past twelve on the morning of March 2nd, Caminada in company with his colleagues, went to the house and apprehended the prisoner. He was in bed. The Chief Detective Inspector told him that he was being taken into custody on suspicion of robbery. He got up and dressed, and was taken to the detective offices.

At day break, Caminada dispatched a number of detectives and police constables to round up witnesses who could identify Parton as the young man. Parton had an alibi ready; he was in Liverpool, at a coursing meeting, on February 26th, and was

THE POLICE INVESTIGATION, MARCH 2ND

at home before six o'clock. However, the Chief Detective Inspector placed him with seven other men, and he was identified by the cabmen Goulding and Coleman, by Emily Pearson from the York Minster, by the policemen Sergeant Allinson and PC Jakeman, and by Thomas Hibbs.

Parton was then charged with having stolen from the person of the deceased gentleman a gold watch and chain of the value of one hundred and twenty pounds, and a sum of money, the amount of which was then unknown.

Caminada immediately contacted the Stipendiary magistrate, Mr Francis Headlam, requesting a hearing before the City Police Court later that Saturday morning. At the hearing, Parton was remanded until Monday, March 4th, pending further police investigation and removed to the cells at the Town Hall.

Back at the cells, the Chief Detective Inspector continued to question Parton who stuck to the story that he was in Liverpool when the crime was committed, attending a coursing meeting. When asked his whereabouts in Liverpool he was very reluctant to mention his location in the city. Eventually he mentioned a particular street; London Road. That rang a bell with Caminada, who immediately returned to his office to search his files. He found what he was looking for; he had previously received a communication about a week earlier from the Liverpool police that a young man was wanted for the theft of a bottle containing one pound of chloral, which he had stolen from a shop in London Road of that city. Caminada was strongly impressed by the fact that the prisoner, Charles Parton, said that he had been at a coursing meeting in the neighbourhood of Liverpool, and should he be the offender, there would at once be an explanation of his possession of the poison used on John Fletcher.

The Chief Detective Inspector took the train to Liverpool on Saturday afternoon and sought an interview with the chemist there. Mr Charles Bromley then informed him of the evidence he would later present at the Coroner's Court on March 5th to the effect that on February 19th previous a young man entered his shop and stole a bottle containing a pound of chloral. Caminada asked the chemist to come to Manchester to identify Parton. This he agreed to do the following day. Upon his arrival, Bromley immediately identified Parton as the man who had stolen the chloral.

The Chief Detective Inspector was now certain that he knew the cause of Fletcher's death. Parton had introduced chloral into the dead man's beer in order to facilitate the robbery. He now awaited the results of the *post-mortem*; the medical men had already been instructed to look for evidence of chloral poisoning.

CHAPTER XIII

The Old Market Place, January 8th

About half-past nine on the evening of January 8th, 1889, a grocer from Ashton-under-Lyne, Mr Samuel Oldfield, walked into the Slip Inn, Blue Boar Court, seeking a little recreation after the toils of the day by partaking of the "free and easy" entertainment. Caminada's memoirs went on to relate that Oldfield had every confidence in himself, could resist temptation, was not likely to be allured by any tempting bait, and, though he had had a few glasses of something to drink during the afternoon, he felt himself a match for every stranger who might tackle him. He knew "a thing or two," and prided himself on being "as fly as they make them." He would be a clever fellow who took him down. So reasoned our grocer on pleasure bent.

As he entered the room a gentleman in the blackest of black coats, plenty of shirt front, white kid gloves, and a good deal of Birmingham jewelry was treating the audience to a song about the "Raging Main." After he had finished, and the rattling of glasses upon the table with which the audience signified their applause was ended, our worthy grocer was addressed by a young stranger who the grocer saw entering the public house during the course of the last song.

"Good song that, governor."

"Rather," answered the careful grocer, as he turned his eyes on the person addressing him.

"I like to hear a song like that; it reminds me of the sea, and I have a brother a sailor," continued the young man.

"Indeed?" was the reply.

"Yes, and I am rather fond of the sea myself; but I am just going to have a glass. Will you have one?"

Now, our grocer could see no objection in having a glass at the young stranger's expense. What could he, a man of the world, have to fear from such an inexperienced child as that, so he replied in the affirmative, and ordered, "a small scotch."

The audience was now treated to one of those old ditties which seem so well adapted in these days to draw money from the pockets of soft-headed people. Whatever defects there were in the music, the touching and exciting nature of the song – of course the theme was the difficulties of two lovers, ending in a solemn tragedy – was certain of an attentive and appreciative audience, and many handkerchiefs were called into requisition by female members of the audience before the story was completed.

"Sup up, governor, and have another," said the innocent young man to his companion, as the song ended. "I am glad our old woman's not here," he continued, as the grocer complied with his request.

"Why? Would she paddle you for taking too much?" dryly remarked the man of the world.

"Oh, no; it's not that. You see, now, our old woman can never hear a song of that sort without breaking her heart, and when I see her shedding tears, it sets me agate too."

"I like you all the better for that," replied the elderly gentleman. "It shows that you have a tender heart, and some respect for the parent who bore you."

"That is so, governor. I have a heart as soft as a pancake. I can't bear to see anything suffer; and as for our old woman, I should like to see them that would touch her; but here comes a singer that all the mashers are sweet on."

The latter remark was made in reference to one of the female singers, whose charm, rouge, and flake had fascinated a number of young mashers, who had been treating her pretty liberally. It is not a beautiful sight to see a row of these young praetorians, with their faultless gloves and exquisitely appointed flower, cudgelling their brains over the libretto of the "Ten Little Niggers"

There sits a thing with pasty cheeks and effeminate habits, that wastes whole days evolving new neckties to suite its complexion. When it enters, lavender or musk impregnates the air. It has not one of the vices of a man. Sympathy it has none, except with its tailor. The one great problem of its life is how to shape its pantaloons.

There sits another individual of the masher type. He may be recognized by his curly hair, his baby lisp, his semi-idiotic grin, his huge cuffs, and, above all, by his never-failing accoutrements – an eyeglass and a stick. Between the latter implement, the proportions of which are of the daintiest possible, and himself there is a mysterious link of sympathy, springing, it maybe, from the mutual consciousness of a common stock.

Near the masher sits young Mumbo-jumbo. Because the office in which he is employed deals in nothing but figures the solemn young coxcomb affects the airs of business. There is a pretence of mathematical precision about his dress and habits. He is always deep in the confidence of his chief, shakes his head in a very mysterious manner, and knows what firms are going wrong long before they know themselves.

But here comes the sweet songstress, and we soon find that she has only about three notes, two at the top and one at the bottom of the scale, which we hear alternately amidst the uproarious applause of her fascinated mashers below.

"Well, what do you think about that, governor?" asked the young innocent of the grocer, after the applause had subsided, and the announcement was made that the lady 'would oblige again.'

"Fine girl, isn't she?" asked the young man.

"Well there's not much amiss," replied the countryman; "but, after all, I don't see what there's about her to take all them young fools in."

"No," replied the young hopeful, "I should put my money to some better use than spend it on a woman I know nothing about, and might never see again."

"That's right young man; take care of your brass; you might want it some day."

"I mean to do, father; but as she is going to sing again, you had better sup up – this is yours."

At the same time he handed to the grocer another glass of whisky, which the latter drank, and after a fit of coughing, the result of the drink remarked, "By gum, young man, that's hot; you've not put much water in it; but I'll pay this time.

The glasses were replenished. The songstress once more appeared, and sang a song with a chorus commencing, "Money is the root of all evil."

"Now," said the young philosopher, at the end of the song, "I don't agree with that; do you, governor?"

"What's that?"

"Why, that money is the root of all evil."

"That depends on how you use it."

"Perhaps it does; but it's a bigger evil to be without it."

"No doubt that's a bad thing; but young fellow, don't you think this whisky's stronger than we've been supping?"

"No, I don't think so; sup it up and have another. Perhaps it is your mouth."

"Perhaps it is," replied the old fellow, as he bottomed the glass, and his youthful friend ordered it to be replenished.

"What I say is this," continued the young philosopher; "if the lady that sung that song had to earn her living at the wash-tub, like our old woman, instead of getting it as easy as she does, and had no swells to treat her, she'd know something about money. Now, don't you think the boot's on the other leg, and that woman's the root of all evil?"

"True," said the old gentleman, shaking his head ominously, probably with some thoughts of what might await him at home; "A vicious woman is a dangerous thing."

The curly-headed masher, however, who heard his charmer compared to a washerwoman, cast upon the speaker one withering glance of contempt, and walked away buttoning his gloves, while the darling stick was suspended under his left arm.

"They are that," replied young precocious; "our old woman's a demon when she starts."

"Is she now? But hand me the water bottle; this whiskey's damned strong," replied his companion.

"I don't think so; you must be getting boozed governor."

"Not I. I can drink twenty yet; but it does not suit my palate."

"Well, let's go somewhere else; there's a first-class pub close to."

This was agreed to, and, drinking up, the two sallied forth arm-in-arm. The country grocer was a fine stout old fellow of between fifty and sixty, and his companion a young stripling of about eighteen, and anyone meeting them might have taken them for father and son.

"Mind what you're doing," said the younger one, as they were entering another public house, the Blue Boar Hotel, "there's always a lot of sharps about here."

"I'm weight for all of that sort," replied the grocer. "You'll see I'll take care of myself."

It was about half-past ten when the two newly-made friends entered the second public house, and here they remained until closing time, when the young innocent volunteered to see his friend to Victoria Station.

Alas for the frailty of human nature! Our strong-minded grocer who "Knew a thing or two," and was well able to take care of himself, remembered leaving the house with his young friend, but as to what occurred afterwards his mind was a complete blank, until he awakened the next morning in a strange and dismal place, which he soon discovered to be a police cell.

On making inquiries of the police he found that he had been locked up for being drunk and incapable, that some charitable young fellow who had found him sitting on some steps beastly drunk in Todd Street, had been kind enough to procure for him a cab, which he ordered to drive to the Cheshire Cheese in Oldham Road. The charitable young man got in at the same time to take care of the poor old gentleman, but had mysteriously disappeared on the way, leaving the object of his charity with his pockets turned inside out.

The cabman, not being able to rouse him, had sought the aid of a policeman, who had driven with him to the police station, whence he had been sent to the Infirmary. At the Infirmary they at first thought he had been poisoned with opium, but after applying the stomach pump came to the conclusion that that he was only beastly drunk, and had him sent back to the lock-ups, so that he was shortly to have the pleasure of appearing before the magistrates to explain his conduct – so becoming to a respectable, staid old gentleman, without having a single penny to pay his fine.

"But my watch and guard?" stammered the old gentleman who "knew a thing or two."

"We know nothing of it; you had no watch and guard when you were brought here," replied the police sergeant.

"But I was wearing it at closing time last night, and had between three and four pounds in my pocket."

"It was all gone, sir, by the time you arrived here. In fact, it would seem that you were driving about without the means of paying the cabman his fare."

"Why did not the cabman drive me home?"

"To the Cheshire Cheese, Oldham Road, he was told, sir."

"Oh, dear, no; I know nothing of the Cheshire Cheese."

"That's where the cabman was ordered to drive, sir."

"Oh, dear, oh, dear; riding about in a cab without money – pockets turned inside out – watch and guard missing – Infirmary – stomach pump – police cell – magistrates – no money to pay the fine – scandal – got to face wife – truly, truly, Sammy, you've learnt a thing or two at last. Oh, my young friend, 'Money is the root of all evil;' that woman's right, and, by gum! I'm feared I shall find out, when I get home that 'a vicious woman is a dangerous thing,' my lad, too."

"What a nice old hairy-headed sinner I am, to be telling that young innocent to take care of his brass, when I cannot take care of my own. The young scamp, to call me father, and talk about his mother, and then send me flying about the town with my pockets picked. Keep out of my road young hopeful, for if I lay my hands on you, I'll break every bone in your body."

"Well, well, Sammy, you've got yourself into a pretty mess by gum; that whisky must have been strong."

Oldfield was brought up before the magistrates and fined 10s. 6d. and costs, or fourteen days, and departed for his home a sadder but a wiser man.

CHAPTER XIV

The Police Investigation, March 3rd

The startling revelations around the Fletcher case that were reported in detail in the local papers on Friday, Saturday and Sunday, resulted in tremendous interest in the affair. Unsolicited information related to the crime now began to flow to Caminada.

On early Sunday morning, March 3rd, a man was reading weekend newspaper reports of the Coroner's Court and City Police Court proceedings and the incident described bore out such a strong resemblance to an experience of his own that he felt convinced that the prisoner was the "nice young man" who had been the cause of his difficulties. "Well my lad," he ruminated, "you have done it once too often. Money with you appears to be the root of all evil still; but the little game has stopped for a bit. Then it wasn't whisky after all. I was drugged was I? By Jingo! I've had a narrow escape; perhaps the stomach pump saved my life. Who knows? But it's too bad to fine a fellow for being drunk when he was poisoned. I wonder if I can get that fine back? But I'll go and see whether they have the right man."

Mr Samuel Oldfield immediately left to go to the Detective Office. There he regaled the Chief Detective Inspector with the Market Place tale detailed in the previous chapter and with much apparent satisfaction picked out Parton, with the exclamation, "Oh, that's him; take him away." He afterwards reminded Mr. Headlam, the Stipendiary magistrate, when giving evidence before him in the case that he had been fined in the same court for being drunk and incapable when in reality he was not drunk, but drugged. He never recovered his fine though!

Caminada checked the files on the incident. The police report indicated that Thomas Robinson was the cabdriver who picked up Oldfield and took him to Goulden Street police station where he was locked up on January 8th, 1889. PC William Doughty along with Robinson took Oldfield from the police station to the Infirmary. The morning following the incident, Doughty visited the Blue Boar Hotel and the barman there, Jessie Mutten, confirmed that two men matching the description of Oldfield and Parton were in the public house drinking the evening before.

The Chief Detective Inspector having reviewed the information immediately sent for Inspector Wilson and dispatched him to the Blue Boar Hotel. There he found Mutten and escourted him back to the Detective Office. Mutten also identified Parton as Oldfield's young drinking companion on the night of January 8th.

Later that same morning, Robert Jackson, a PC working in the Detective Office, came into Caminada's office to remind him of an incident that occurred in December the previous year. On the morning of December 29th, 1888, a railway porter from Ashton-under-Lyne, called Parkey, came into the Detective Office to complain of an incident that occurred the evening before. The complaint was that, later detailed by Parkey at the City Police Court on March 8th, to the effect that he and his friend met the prisoner and his brother and he ended up being drugged in the Crown and Anchor. Jackson told Caminada that the following day he proceeded to the Crown and Anchor to interview the barman. Alfred Moxon confirmed serving four men the previous evening and that Parkey became quite stupefied.

On the afternoon of the same day, a young man called John Wittaker called on the Chief Detective Inspector. He too had been reading newspaper reports and knew Charles Parton. He was staying in the same house as Parton and was there when Parton was arrested by the police on March 2nd. He also mentioned that on the evening of February 26th he saw Parton return home with an expensive gold watch and plenty of money. He saw Parton pass the watch and some money to his father, "Pig Jack," but kept some coins for himself which he hid under his mattress.

Parkey, Coxon and the Parton brothers left the White Bear Inn and proceeded to the Crown and Anchor.

Having heard this, Caminada called for Detective Sergeants Harris and Schofield, both who had assisted in the arrest of Parton, and sent them back to 12, Moore Street, Rochdale Road. There they found two sovereigns hidden in the straw mattress of the prisoner's bed.

CHAPTER XV

The Police Investigation, March 11th and 13th

Following the committal of Parton for trial by the City Police Court on Friday, March 8th, the pressure was very much on Caminada. The case against Parton was largely circumstantial and Caminada needed more evidence if he was to secure a conviction. Consequently, in the interval between the committal and the trial, he continued to interview witnesses and investigate the crime in an effort to establish more evidence against the prisoner. He found two additional witnesses, one of whom could be crucial in obtaining a conviction. This was Andrew Phillips.

On Monday morning, March 11th, the Chief Detective Inspector received a visit at the Detective Office from a Mr Alan Yates, manager of the London Dress Company. Yates proceeded to tell Caminada that he had received some information from one of his employees related to the Fletcher case. In response to an inquiry from Caminada, Yates explained that, "We have an employee, Andrew Phillips, engaged as a book-keeper. Late on Friday last he came to see me. He was disturbed. Something had happened which he worried might effect his job with us. Eventually, he told me the problem. He was in the Three Arrows when Fletcher was there that Tuesday night and knows something about the incident. He has been following reports in the newspapers. What he saw on Tuesday night that he then thought harmless, he now considers may be more significant to the case. He has been reluctant to come forward since he thinks we, his employer, would take a very dim view of him drinking in public houses such as the Three Arrows. After he had finished telling me, I indicated that he need not be concerned about his job. I decided to call on you on my way to work this morning in case this information is of value."

Caminada asked, "Do you know what Phillips saw?"

Yates replied, "He saw the younger of the two men pour some fluid from a small phial into a glass of beer on that Tuesday night in the Three Arrows."

Caminada continued, "Is Phillips at work today?"

"Yes, he should be," replied Yates.

"Then with your permission I will go and see him forthwith."

The two then walked over to the London Dress Company located just a few minutes walk on Deansgate, not far from the Three Arrows. Yates took the Detective Chief Inspector to the ledger room in which the accountants worked and introduced him to the Chief Accountant. The latter took him over to Phillips' desk. The Chief Detective Inspector took him to one side and asked, "Were you in the public house when Fletcher and his young companion were there?" He reluctantly admitted that he was.

Caminada continued, "Did you see anything unusual occur?"

Phillips, again, reluctantly replied, "Yes."

"Did you see someone pour some fluid from a small phial into a glass of beer."

"I did."

Phillips agreed to proceed to the detective office where he gave a witness statement before PC Miller detailing what he had observed at the Three Arrows. He was later taken to the cells and identified Charles Parton as the person involved.

The second witness that the Chief Detective Inspector found was Samuel Heywood. On Wednesday March 13th, the Chief Detective Inspector was visited by a gentleman, who was an India-rubber manufacturer and knew Fletcher well. Heywood began, "The reason I am here is that on the evening of February 26th, about a quarter to seven o'clock, I was passing the Three Arrows and saw Fletcher and the young man leaving. I called out to Fletcher who just looked at me in a funny way and did not respond. However, I have been following the case in the newspapers and came to the conclusion that Fletcher could have been behaving the way he was, because he had been drugged in the Three Arrows, and was beginning to feel the effects as he was leaving with Parton to get in the cab."

The Chief Detective Inspector then took Heywood to see Parton whom he readily identified as the young man with whom Fletcher was leaving the Three Arrows as he passed by.

PART THREE
THE TRIAL

CHAPTER XVI

The Trial, Day One, March 18th, The Case for the Prosecution

On Monday, March 18th, 1889, at the Liverpool Assizes, Charles Parton was put on trial before Mr Justice Charles, charged with the murder of John Fletcher. Council for the prosecution were Mr C. H. Hopwood, Q.C., Recorder of Liverpool, and Mr Shee. The prisoner was defended by Mr C. P. McKeand and Mr Jordan. Mr Overend Evans held a watching brief over the proceedings on behalf of the relatives of the deceased.

Mr Justice Charles. Image of the Trial Judge published in the Liverpool Echo *Monday March 18th, 1889.*

Extraordinary interest was manifested in the case. The Court met at half-past ten, but some time before that hour a considerable crowd had gathered in the steps and in the vicinity of St George's Hall, and there was much pressure when the doors of the Crown Court were opened. Though many hundreds were refused admission the Court was crowded all day, and the greatest interest was taken in the proceedings.

The prisoner was placed in the dock about a quarter to eleven. He was described in the calendar as being eighteen years of age. His appearance had altered little; he was again neatly attired in a tweed suit.

THE TRIAL, DAY ONE, MARCH 18TH, THE CASE FOR THE PROSECUTION

The first indictment against the prisoner set forth that, "At the city of Manchester on the 8th of January, 1889, Charles Parton unlawfully and feloniously did administer to Samuel Oldfield a certain stupefying drug called chloral with intent thereby to enable him, the said Charles Parton, to commit a certain indictable offence, to wit, to steal from the person of the said Samuel Oldfield one watch and guard, value £10, and certain moneys, his property, and with having on the same day and year, at the said city, feloniously stolen from the person of the said Samuel Oldfield one watch and chain and certain moneys, his property."

The second indictment set forth that, "At the city of Manchester, on the 26h of February, 1889, Charles Parton feloniously and wilfully and of malice aforethought did kill and slay one John Fletcher, and on the day and in the city aforesaid unlawfully and feloniously did administer to the said John Fletcher a certain stupefying drug called chloral with intent thereby to render him insensible, to enable him to commit a certain indictable offense, to wit, to steal from the person of the said John Fletcher, a watch and guard, and certain moneys, his property; with having on the day and year, and at the city aforesaid, feloniously stolen from the said John Fletcher, one watch and guard, value £100, and certain moneys, his property; and with having on the 19th of February, at Liverpool, feloniously stolen one bottle and one pound weight of chloral, the property of Charles Bromley."

A third indictment set forth that, "At the city of Manchester, on the 28th of December, 1888, Charles Parton unlawfully and feloniously did administer to one John Parkey a certain stupefying drug called chloral, with intent thereby to enable him to commit a certain indictable offence, to wit, to steal from the said John Parkey one watch and one chain and 18s. 6d. in money, his property, and with having on the day and the year at the city aforesaid, stolen from the person of the said John Parkey one watch and chain and 18s. 6d. in money, his property."

The second indictment was the one the Court proceeded to try. When arraigned on this capital charge the prisoner pleaded, "Not guilty," in a low voice.

Hopwood opened the case for the prosecution. He said to the jury, "You are about to undertake an inquiry of a very painful character. The young man at the bar is charged with the wilful murder founded upon certain circumstances attendant upon the death of a Mr John Fletcher. It is impossible to keep from your minds the fact that the case requires very close attention. It has been the subject of comment, and the facts might have reached the ears of some of you, but in all these matters it is necessary to remember that if publicity was no disadvantage to the prisoner it was an advantage to the prosecution. Several instances will occur in the course of the trial which will demonstrate that publicity has been useful to the ends of justice. However, I caution you against yielding to any preconceived notions with regard to the facts of the case. You are gentlemen assembled under the sanction of the law to try a fellow citizen upon a grave charge and I am sufficiently persuaded of your general fairness of conduct to trust you to the task.

"The unfortunate gentleman whose death you are about to inquire into was a paper manufacturer, living at Southport, and he was recently elected upon the County Council for that district. He had to a great measure retired from active participation in his business, and left matters largely to his partner, Mr Robert Fletcher, a nephew. He was found in a cab on the point of death, and he was conveyed to the Infirmary at Manchester, and his death occurred as he was being taken from the cab into that institution.

Mr Hopwood, recorder. Image of Trial Council for the Prosecution published in the Liverpool Echo Monday March 18th, 1889.

"It is upon these circumstances that the whole facts of the case which I will lay before you are centred. I will describe to you first the earlier incidents of the case, which will develop into two or three parts. Mr Fletcher, who was at the time in his usual health, went to Manchester on the 26th of February last, and visited his office in New Cannon Street, where he saw his nephew, Mr Robert Fletcher. After some conversation with Mr. Robert Fletcher he left his office and intimated that he was going to the Mitre Hotel, situated not far from the Cathedral, in Manchester, in order to attend the sale of a mill. Accordingly, somewhere around 1:30 pm, he left his nephew. This was the last which Mr Robert Fletcher saw of his uncle alive. He saw him next morning at the Infirmary, and identified the body. The next opportunity we have of tracing Mr John Fletcher's movements after he left his nephew was when he appeared at the Mitre Hotel. It was then somewhere near 5 o'clock. What he might

THE TRIAL, DAY ONE, MARCH 18TH, THE CASE FOR THE PROSECUTION

have done in the interval I am unable to say, but it seems at the hotel he met several friends. At that time he appeared in his usual health. One of these friends has described Mr Fletcher as at that time under the influence of drink and another has spoken of him being sober. These accounts are doubtless reconcilable by the persons who had expressed these opinions, and it seems clear that Mr Fletcher, although he had evidently been drinking, was in full possession of his faculties and was able to conduct himself as a man in good health. After remaining some time and having a social drink with his friends, Mr. Fletcher left, stating that he was going to Sinclair's, a shop where many people go to get luncheon and refreshment, in Victoria Market. It was then, of course, past the hour of luncheon, but one of the gentlemen promised to meet him there. That gentleman did not appear but I will show that Mr Fletcher was outside that shop. He did not appear to have taken anything there, but he was seen by the people who kept the shop to be in conversation with a young man.

That young man, the evidence will show, is the prisoner at the bar. Where he met with Mr Fletcher, or what the inducement to enter into conversation was, or whether they had known one another previously, I cannot say, but it seems that after talking for some time the prisoner called a cab. A police officer called Jakeman, who was on the spot, saw the two get into it and has spoken positively to the identity of the prisoner as the man who got in with Mr Fletcher. The cabman who has also spoken positively as to the identity of the prisoner said that he received from the prisoner directions to drive to the Three Arrows public house, a very short distance up Deansgate in Manchester. The Three Arrows public house is situated at the corner of St Mary's Street and Deansgate, with a side door a little way down St Mary's Street. There they got out and remained, according to different statements, for ten to twenty minutes.

"At this point, one of the witnesses has deposed to a very remarkable circumstance. At the time it appears there were five or six gentlemen in the house, and two of these – Mr Phillips and Mr Heywood – will be called as witnesses. Mr. Phillips is a witness who was not previously before the Court. He was present on the occasion, but although there passed to his knowledge something which he has since disclosed to the police, he, being a bookkeeper to a respectable firm in Manchester, was naturally a little unwilling to come forward from the circumstance that he was taking his social glass in a public house. He has stated that the two, Mr Fletcher and the prisoner, were near to one another, and that he saw distinctly the prisoner with a small phial in his hand. He will describe to you how he poured something into a glass, which he thought was a glass of beer. He said, fairly enough, he did not see the glasses changed, and probably you will think that he had no suspicion of anything being wrong. What came to his mind was the thought that the prisoner was getting himself some medicine or taking something to moderate the affects of the beer he had been drinking. Hence, no suspicion crossed his mind until he saw the narration in the public prints of the extraordinary inquiry. In consequence of that, information was given, and he will be a witness here today. This is the first important matter against the prisoner at the bar.

"We do not know how many glasses of beer were drunk, but it did not appear that any spirits were taken. What will be shown next is that Mr Fletcher and the prisoner left the house together to go and get into the cab again. Mr Fletcher is described by the earlier witnesses I have mentioned as wearing a valuable gold watch and a valuable heavy gold curb chain and you should presume and assume that he had those articles on him when he entered the Three Arrows.

"The next piece of evidence I should lay before you is that of a gentleman who knew Mr Fletcher well and who was passing the Three Arrows at the time that Mr Fletcher and the prisoner were crossing the pavement to get into the cab. Though the witness said he did not notice the cab he saw Mr Fletcher and addressed him. Mr Fletcher looked at him in a funny way, but did not respond, and he then passed on without continuing his endeavour to make Mr Fletcher recognize him or to speak to him. It is possible that if something was given to Mr Fletcher in the Three Arrows, as a witness I already described to you claims, it might have already begun to have its effect. At all events, Mr Fletcher was able to walk from the Three Arrows to the cab and to get in, and then the prisoner gave to the cabman directions to drive to 43, Stretford Road. I will call before you the tradesman who keeps the lock-up shop there, and he will tell you he knows nothing of Mr Fletcher or the prisoner, and could not understand why they should come to him. The object would be, if the suspicions of the prosecution and our suggestions against the prisoner are well founded, to obtain a sufficiently long cab ride under an excuse to enable him to perpetrate the robbery with which he is charged. The same gentleman who saw Mr Fletcher and spoke to him outside the Three Arrows, saw that at that time he was wearing his watch chain, and presumably his watch. They got into the cab, and after they had proceeded rather more than half-way towards Stretford Road, there was a little obstruction by a procession or something of that sort, and the cabman came to a walking pace.

"His attention was then called by some passer by to the fact that someone had got out of his cab. He looked down and saw his cab door was open. He got down and found to his surprise that there was only one person in the cab, and that person was Mr. John Fletcher. The prisoner had in fact gone, and from that time Mr Fletcher's watch, chain and purse were missing. He found Mr Fletcher in a state of collapse sitting on what the cabman calls the back seat with his head forward upon the front. The cabman endeavoured to rouse him, but could get nothing from him, but some expression of begging to be left alone. Accordingly, the cabman, with difficulty and in trouble, finally drove back to the place where he had taken up the two men, as likely to be the only place where he could learn some news. He did not know Mr Fletcher and did not know where to take him, and accordingly he came back to the Cathedral, where he had taken up the two men, and he found there the same constable who had

THE TRIAL, DAY ONE, MARCH 18TH, THE CASE FOR THE PROSECUTION

seen the two men get into the cab. He drew this constable's attention to Mr Fletcher's unfortunate state, and the officer thinking him intoxicated directed the cabman to drive him to one of the police stations. In a short time, however, the constable became alarmed at the condition of Mr Fletcher, and seeing now that it was not an ordinary drunken case, he directed the cabman to drive to the Infirmary. It appears that the unfortunate man expired whilst in the act of being taken into the Infirmary. He was received by Dr Hampden-Barker who will describe to you what measures he took in the case. The man was unfortunately dead, but the doctor suspecting poison, took certain precautions which he will detail to you.

"I now come to another remarkable fact. I have shown you so far *prima facie* evidence, that there was a possibility at least, and a probability, though the probability might be uncertain in your minds, that to Mr Fletcher there had been unlawfully administered something which, judging from subsequent circumstances, you will, after you had heard all, feel clearly proved, had taken away his powers, and in fact destroyed his life. Now, is the prisoner the man who had administered that something? Was he in possession of anything deadly that might have affected so terrible a result upon the life of Mr Fletcher? These events occurred on the 26th of February, and on the 19th, in Liverpool, a remarkable scene in connection with this trial took place. Mr Charles Bromley is a chemist and druggist keeping a shop in London Road in that city, and on the evening of the 19th of February, there came into his shop a young man whose request was for forty grains of chloral. The chemist, naturally cautious, said that they do not give such a large quantity as that and they do not give chloral except under prescription. The young man besought him, and at last the chemist consented to let him have ten grains on the plea that the young man's mother was suffering from *angina pectoris*. The chemist took a pound bottle from the shelf and placed it perhaps incautiously upon his counter, and whilst he was proceeding to dispense the small quantity of ten grains, the young man snatched up the pound bottle and ran out of the shop. The chemist pursued him and shouted after him, but all his endeavours were ineffectual to capture him. The chemist will tell you that he has no doubt whatever that it was the prisoner's hand that stole the bottle.

"I might mention here a coincidence which perhaps will be valuable in your eyes in connection with this disease of *angina pectoris* which is perhaps a medical term which did not often come within the range of people in the prisoner's class of life. It is a remarkable fact that a short time since, the prisoner's father was at the Manchester Infirmary under treatment for *angina pectoris*, and hence it might be that the prisoner had learned the term, became familiar with it and associated it with the administration of chloral, and so was enabled to use the knowledge with the chemist. I offer this to you as worthy of your consideration, for if there is any necessity for the corroboration of Mr Bromley's evidence, this will be corroboration itself.

"After the unfortunate gentleman had been taken to the Infirmary, I will carry the narrative further and tell you what became of the prisoner. He escaped from the cab to a public house called the York Minster, in Higher Chatham Street, which is not a great way from No. 43, Stretford Road, to which place, as I have told you, the prisoner gave the cabman directions to drive. At the public house he seems to have stayed for some little time, and there got change for some halfpence. He is described by one witness as being 'put about' when he came in, and, indeed, I think he used the word 'flabbergasted.' He explains it by saying that there was something about the prisoner indicating that he seemed put out, as if something had occurred to agitate him. He said further that the prisoner, while there, pulled out of his pocket a handful of money – halfpence, silver and gold – and proceeded to separate the gold from the silver and halfpence, and put it away in separate pockets. He had also a large and valuable gold watch and chain upon him, and he produced them, and asked about the time and compared it. He had also this peculiarity that he asked for a cab when he could have gone for one himself. They said to him, 'You will get one at All Saints' church, which is at the top of Stretford Road,' a short distance from where they were. The prisoner, however, said he did not know the place, that he was a stranger there, and that he had just come from London. All these statements are very remarkable and when placed together it is for you to say what effect is produced upon your minds. A cab was got, and the prisoner paid something to the man who got it, and he then got on the cab along with the cabman. There is no doubt to his identity, because a police sergeant met the cab and saw the prisoner outside. He had seen the prisoner at some boxing exhibition or something of that sort, at the Free Trade Hall, and he knew the cabman also. The cabman remarked that the prisoner was 'shaky,' and he induced him to get down and get into the cab, and helped to cover him with a rug. Of course if the prisoner had left the deceased man Fletcher in a state of collapse, although possibly he might not have intended so tragical a result, it followed upon what he had been doing – having as you are asked to believe been administering a drug – that he might be shaky afterwards. It is also a circumstance for your consideration whether the prisoner was not trying to fence around all traces of himself by saying he was a stranger and came from London. Some short time afterwards the prisoner was taken into custody by Chief Detective Inspector Caminada, who very properly warned him to say nothing. He was placed among other persons and shown to the witnesses in that way and he was immediately and completely identified. His story is that he was home at six o'clock, and that he had been at some coursing. Whether that statement is reconcilable with the facts I will show through the witnesses.

"The prisoner is defended by able and learned counsel and it is a great relief to my mind that that is so, and that you will give him the benefit of your valuable services. I, however, have a further slight matter to state. The police were seen by a man named Wittaker when they arrested the prisoner. Wittaker later made a communication to the police who went again to the place where the prisoner was arrested, and they found concealed under the mattress in his bedroom two sovereigns. I desire to ask upon the facts I have opened whether in your minds there will be any doubt that Mr Fletcher came by his death in consequence of something administered to him by the prisoner, he being shown to be in possession of a deadly agent.

"Dr Hampden-Barker and Dr Reynolds, who saw the deceased at the Royal Infirmary, will describe the condition in which they found the deceased. The medical testimony will show that there was nothing in the condition of the deceased to account for death. The symptoms and *post-mortem* appearance exactly corresponded with death as a result of succumbing to the effects of chloral.

"Now, an aspersion has been cast upon the character of the deceased that he indulged far too freely in liquors. It is a question as to how this circumstance, if true, coincided with the appearance of the deceased, and as to how far that might have had its effect in connection with the administration of a drug. The medical men believe that there was nothing in the disease of the heart that caused his death. It might be that that disease might go on, and it might be a question of days or months, but there was nothing to account for death. It is possible, in the ingenuity of the learned gentlemen who defend the prisoner, that it might be suggested that a man who was diseased about the heart was more likely to succumb to the influence of a deadly drug than a man who was perfectly healthy. That matters not to me representing justice, nor to you as inquirers in the interest of justice. If the prisoner by his acts accelerated Mr Fletcher's death by a single day he is guilty of murder. It matters not what other causes might combine to cause death, and it matters not whether the unfortunate man was, to some extent, the worse for drink before the drug was administered. He was in his usual state of health, and whether the fact that he was in drink, or whether the fact that he was to some extent diseased internally, formed a fertile ground upon which poison may take effect was immaterial, if his death was accelerated by that poison it is murder.

"You will get much more authoritative direction from his Lordship. But I feel called upon to point out that the two medical gentlemen agree that syncope was the cause of death. That was the sort of result they would expect from the administration of chloral. The effect of chloral almost infallibly is to leave the blood in a state of fluidity, and that was the condition of the deceased gentleman's blood at the time of the *post-mortem*. In the case of coma the blood is in a state of coagulation. The city analyst of Manchester, who had made a careful examination in this matter, and who used the most difficult tests, had found traces of chloral in the intestines of the deceased. Thus you have the prisoner in possession of chloral, you have the fact of the prisoner pouring something into the glass, and you have the subsequent effects of chloral upon the deceased in the cab; finally you have traces of chloral in the body. On these facts you will have to come to your verdict."

CHAPTER XVII

The Trial, Day One, March 18th, The Prosecution Witnesses

Hopwood continued, "I will now call my first witness."

Henry Goulding, Mary Frost, George Wild, William Hall and Edward Lait were called in sequence and all repeated the evidence they had given in the earlier part of the judicial inquiry at Manchester.

Robert Fletcher, repeated the identification evidence he previously presented to the Coroner's Court on March 1st. He added that his uncle usually came to Manchester once or twice a week and had been in good health. As far as he knew, his uncle was not acquainted with the prisoner. He was a generous man, kind in many ways and was in the habit of treating people to drink when under the influence, but he was not in the habit of speaking to strangers.

McKeand cross-examined the witness by asking, "Can you describe your uncle's drinking habits and health?"

Fletcher replied, "My uncle occasionally took too much drink but I have never remonstrated with him about this. He was a big stout man about 6 ft. in height, but during the last twelve or fifteen months he had got thinner. I believe he suffered slightly from heart disease."

Hopwood interjected, "You do not know for a fact that he suffered from heart disease. That is merely your layman's opinion." Fletcher concurred with the statement.

Police Constable Jakeman repeated the evidence he had given before the Coroner's Court on March 1st. McKeand then asked Jakeman, "In order to get to Stretford Road would the cab have to be driven through well-lighted streets."

"I believe so," replied the police constable.

The first piece of new evidence was introduced when Andrew Phillips was called. Phillips, a bookkeeper from Manchester, said, "I was in the Three Arrows on the 26th of February last. In the room where I was there were half a dozen other people, and among them I noticed the prisoner in company with an elderly gentleman of stout build and pretty tall. I noticed them directly after they came in, which I would say was between a quarter to seven and seven o'clock. The two were in conversation, both had glasses of beer before them and were sitting between two tables. After the glasses came I saw the prisoner empty the contents of a small

Image of John Fletcher published in the Liverpool Echo *Monday March 18, 1889.*

round bottle which he had in his hand into one of the glasses. I saw all this distinctly because the prisoner and his companion were seated in a corner of the room and I was facing them. The prisoner held the bottle between his two fingers and emptied the contents into his own glass. Some little time after, the prisoner held the two glasses up as if looking through them. He then put them down again but I did not see him change them. Before they left I made an observation to the landlady. I did not offer to prevent the prisoner acting as he did since the thought that struck me at the time was that the prisoner was taking some medicine."

In response to a further question by Hopwood, as to why he had not come forward sooner, Phillips responded, "Detective Inspector Caminada afterwards came and told me of the present inquiry. I have come forward reluctantly. When the case was investigated in the Police Court I was present but gave no evidence. I went to the Police Office in consequence of Detective Inspector Caminada calling upon me, but I went previously to the Police Court and of my own accord to satisfy myself that the prisoner was the man I had seen at the Three Arrows."

Phillips was then subjected to extensive cross-examination by McKeand. Under such questioning, he said that he was employed by the London Dress Company in Deansgate, Manchester, and had been there about two years. He went to the Three Arrows between a quarter and half-past six. When the prisoner and the old gentleman came in he had had one glass of beer and remained in the public house until about a quarter to eight. The colour of the liquid in the bottle which the prisoner had he did not see. The bottle was a white one, but whether it had in it a stopper or a cork he could not say. It was about as thick round as his thumb. He knew nothing of chloral, and could not say what colour it was. When the prisoner took up his glass he had it on the left side of him, and was apparently quite sober.

McKeand then asked, "You saw the liquid going into the glass?"

Phillips responded, "Yes."

"And you could not tell the colour?"

"No."

"But you were watching?"

"Yes."

"How far off?"

"About three yards. He had the glass in his right hand, and the bottle in his left."

"You were three yards away, and you saw him pour it into the glass, and yet you cannot tell me the colour of it. Do you really mean to say that?"

"If I were really asked to express myself, I should say it was a yellow colour, not white. The liquid poured in was lighter than beer."

"But chloral is colourless, not yellow at all. Anyway, what was Mr Fletcher doing the whole time this was being poured into his glass?"

"He was talking to the prisoner."

"He was talking to the prisoner, watching him pour the stuff into his glass?"

"No. He did not see what he was doing. He had it between his fingers, and it was impossible for Mr Fletcher to see."

"How long did the operation of pouring this in last?"

"A very few seconds."

"Did you see what he did with the bottle?"

"I did. He put it into his overcoat pocket."

"Did it not strike you when he was doing something which Mr Fletcher could not see that he was doing something which he did not want Mr Fletcher to see?"

"It did not."

"Did it not strike you also that it was an odd thing for a man to be taking medicine in beer? Did you ever hear of a man taking medicine in beer?"

"No."

"You say you saw the prisoner holding the two glasses up to look at. There was no doubt which glass the liquid was in?"

"He put it in his own glass."

"He held both up to the gaslight in the presence of Mr Fletcher, with Mr Fletcher looking at the operation?"

"Yes."

"How many people were in the house at the time?"

"About six besides myself."

"Had they an opportunity of observing what you saw?"

"No, because I only was in a position to see."

"Had they opportunities of seeing the man hold up the glasses in his right hand?"

"Yes."

"Had they an opportunity of seeing that he was doing something with his left hand?"

"No."

"Why not?"

"Because he held the glass on his knee."

"Do you mean to say that a man, if he had been looking, could not have seen this operation going on?"

"I should say so."

"And had not all persons in the room an equal opportunity of seeing what took place?"

"Certainly."

"Did not the fact of a man putting liquid into his own beer, and then holding the two glasses up to the light, arouse your suspicions? Did you not think something was wrong?"

"No, because he put it into his own glass."

"Your suspicions must have been aroused. Why did you not mention it to Mr. Fletcher? Answer that question."

Hopwood interjected, "I submit the witness ought to be allowed to say what he did see."

McKeand stated, "If your Lordship thinks I am wrong in putting these questions…"

"I think you are quite right", interrupted Justice Charles.

McKeand continued his cross examination, "I asked you a plain question. If you thought there was something wrong why did you not mention it to the deceased man?"

"Because he put it in his own glass."

"After you left the public house who was the first person to whom you mentioned what you had seen?"

Phillips initially replied, "I do not recollect," but then corrected himself, "it was my wife."

McKeand continued, "That was after you had seen it in the papers?"

"Yes."

"After you had been to the Police Court to satisfy yourself?"

"No."

"Had you heard at the time that a man had been drugged in the Three Arrows?"

"No."

"Then I ask you this. Not having heard that a man had been drugged in the Three Arrows, why should you mention anything about a man taking medicine in the Three Arrows public house to your wife?"

"From the simple fact that I knew the party I had seen there answer to the description I had read in the papers."

"Then I misunderstood you. Did you tell anybody else besides your wife?"

"Not to my recollection."

"Did you go to the Police Court, did you see Parton there and did you satisfy yourself that he was the young man you had seen in the company of Mr Fletcher.

"I did."

"Now, having satisfied yourself as to the identity of this young man, knowing the terrible charge made against him, and knowing the importance of the evidence you have given today, I ask you why did you not mention it to Mr Caminada then?"

"I did not think what I saw was sufficient evidence."

"But did it not strike you to tell Caminada in the interests of justice and let the police judge whether it was good evidence or not?"

"I did not want to be mixed up in a case of this kind."

"Why didn't you tell me that at first? Did you tell your employers having seen this?"

"Yes."

"And was it in consequence of what you told your employers that Mr Caminada came?"

"I don't know."

"And you mean to tell the jury that unless Caminada had found this out and come and asked you about it you never would have given evidence in the case at all?"

"Yes."

"You mean to say that?"

"Yes."

"Although you knew the terrible charge had been made you would have kept your tongue between your teeth. That is so is it?"

"I have my own interests to look after."

"I dare say you have your own interests. Have your masters or employers ever threatened you with dismissal because you have been speaking the truth, if you are speaking the truth?"

"No."

"When was it Caminada came to speak to you?"

"I think it was this day week."

"Had there been two hearings before the magistrates and three hearings before the coroner?"

"Yes."

"You had read the reports in the daily papers?"

"I had."

"No doubt with great interest, Mr Phillips?"

"Well, yes."

"Did Caminada first of all put a question to you?"

"No, he put a statement to me."

"Was it a written one?"

"No, a verbal one."

"To the effect that you had seen what you have stated today?"

"Yes."

"To some parts of the statement Caminada put to you, you said "Ay," and to some you said, 'No.'"

"Yes."

"There were some parts you had not seen?"

"Yes."

"And you could not swear to what you had seen?"

"No."

"Then you were taken down to the Police Office and had to make a written statement there?"

"Yes."

"Whom before?"

"Mr Miller."

"He put no questions to you, and you simply made your statement?"

"Yes."

"Which he took down in writing?"

"Yes."

"And you signed it?"

"Yes."

At this point McKeand completed his cross-examination and the court was adjourned for luncheon. On resuming, after the interval, Hopwood called Samuel Heywood. He said, "I am an India-rubber manufacturer and knew the late Mr. Fletcher well. On the evening of the 26th of February, about a quarter to seven o'clock, I was passing the Three Arrows and saw Fletcher and the young man leaving. I called out to Fletcher who just looked at me in a funny way and did not respond. I'm not even sure he recognized me. I then passed on without continuing to endeavour to make Mr Fletcher recognize me or to speak to me."

Frank Spedding, Harry Smith, Emily Pearson, Andrew Holt, William Coleman, Detective Sergeant Allinson and Charles Bromley then sequentially presented the evidence they had previously given in the earlier part of the judicial inquiry at Manchester.

Chief Detective Inspector Caminada spoke to taking the prisoner into custody. Detective Sergeant Harris and Detective Sergeant Schofield gave evidence as to the apprehension of the prisoner and to subsequently finding two sovereigns under the prisoner's bed.

Dr John Hampden-Barker described the condition of the body on his arrival at the institution and also the result of the post mortem examination. He said syncope, from which the deceased died, might be caused by alcohol or some other poison.

Hopwood then asked, "The deceased was able to walk into the cab at the Cathedral, and also after he left the Three Arrows. Ten minutes or a quarter of an hour afterwards he was in a helpless state. In your opinion is that a symptom attending alcoholic poisoning or chloral poisoning?"

Hampden-Barker replied, "It very much more resembles the symptoms of chloral poisoning, but still alcohol cannot be absolutely excluded. I think the probability is exceedingly great that the man died from the effects of chloral coupled with alcohol, but he may have died from alcohol. The possibility that he had died from alcohol alone though is very small."

Under cross-examination Hampden-Barker was asked, "What is the smallest quantity of chloral that would cause death?"

In response to McKeand's question, the witness said, "I cannot state what is the smallest quantity of chloral that would cause death. Twenty grains of chloral have been known to prove fatal, but on the other hand, 160 or 180 grains have been taken without death resulting. The present is the first case of death to come under my notice occasioned by chloral poisoning. However, in all reported cases of chloral poisoning the blood of the deceased was in a fluid state, as Mr Fletcher's was."

McKeand then asked, "Up to the time you made the *post-mortem* examination had you any reason to suppose that this man might have poisoned himself by alcohol?"

"We had," replied Hampden-Barker.

"You are in a position to say that that was not so?"

"No, not definitely; but we suspected something. There was no solid food in his stomach. A man who took alcohol without solid food would be more liable to alcoholic poisoning than a man who had his meals regularly. There was a slight trace of fatty degeneration of the heart, and a man in that condition was more likely to be affected by drink than a man who was healthy. If I had not been informed that a trace of chloral had been found, I would have formed the opinion that Mr Fletcher had died from alcoholic poisoning."

"This man might have died from alcoholic poisoning?"

"He may."

"You cannot say he did not?"

"Not absolutely."

Hopwood interjected, "Is it probable he died of alcoholic poisoning?"

"It is not."

Dr Reynolds, medical officer at the Infirmary, detailed at length the result of the *post-mortem* examination of the body. After having heard the whole of the evidence, assuming that chloral was found in the stomach, it was his opinion that death was due to the administration of chloral.

In answer to McKeand's cross-examination asking about the general health of Fletcher, the witness said the deceased had undoubtedly had pleurisy at some time, and had also been in the habit of consuming considerable quantities of liquor. He had what was known as a gin drinker's liver in its early stages.

McKeand then asked, "Was it possible for a gentleman to have walked out of the Three Arrows and got into the cab and died from alcoholic poisoning only?"

"I could not say it was impossible, but it was highly improbable, according to my experience."

"I will put it a different way, as it is a question of life and death to the prisoner. You would not like to say that Mr Fletcher has not died from alcoholic poisoning?"

"I won't swear that Mr Fletcher did not die from alcoholic poisoning."

The Court was then adjourned until ten o'clock the next morning. Throughout the day, while outwardly maintaining an air of calmness and even unconcern, it was evident that Parton paid deep attention to the proceedings. The gravity of the charge which was preferred against him, however, had greatly altered his demeanour. During the early stages of the inquiry at Manchester he assumed a careless, jaunty air, and occasionally looked round to exchange a smile of recognition with his friends, but throughout this day he was very grave. Seated on a chair in front of the dock he paid careful attention to the evidence, and on one or two occasions whispered to his counsel, McKeand, who was seated immediately in front of him.

CHAPTER XVIII

The Trial, Day Two, March 19th, The Medical Evidence.

The trial of Charles Parton continued on Tuesday, March 19th, at the Liverpool Assizes. It was generally expected that the case would terminate early in the afternoon, and the desire of the general public to gain an entrance to the court to witness the closing scenes of a remarkable trial was very widespread. As a result the approaches to the court were thronged at an early hour, and the police had an arduous duty in regulating admission. The court was soon uncomfortably crowded, and there were an unusual number of ladies present. The jury, who had passed the night at an adjacent hotel, entered their box shortly before ten o'clock, and upon the judge taking his seat as the clock struck the hour, the prisoner was placed at the bar and again provided with a chair.

Hopwood first recalled Dr Reynolds with permission of the judge, and asked him about the prisoner's father, who had been a patient in the Infirmary under Dr Reynolds' care, suffering from *angina pectoris*. He was there, said the doctor, for about two months, and he was discharged about six weeks or two months before February 26th.

Mr Charles Estcourt, public analyst for the City of Manchester, was next examined. He received three jars and explained the process of analysis. He made three tests of the contents of the jars with the especial view of discovering the presence of chloroform or chloral.

His Lordship questioned Estcourt at some length in explanation of the process of analysis he had pursued and took copious notes. The witness' conclusion was that chloral was present in the contents of the stomach and in the intestines.

Hopwood then asked, "Did you make more than one test of the contents of the stomach?"

"I made three by the same means, and the results were the same."

Cross-examined by McKeand, the witness was asked, "Why did you test for chloral?"

Estcourt replied, "I was told by the Coroner's Office to examine the contents of the jars for chloral hydrate. The chloroform I obtained by the process I have described, results from the decomposition of chloral."

The Judge then commented, "In his evidence before the Coroner he said, 'all the jars had an alcoholic smell, but he could detect no smell of chloral.'"

McKeand asked the witness, "The process is an extremely delicate one, is it not?"

"It is said to be, but I have never found is so."

"But before the Coroner you described it as an 'exceedingly delicate' test."

"I might have said the word 'delicate,' but certainly not the word 'exceedingly.'"

"You use the word 'trace'; what do you mean by that word?"

"I mean that I found such a small quantity that I could not get it out to weigh it. I could only indicate its presence. There are various degrees of traces, but this is what an analyst would call a trace."

"Would it be possible for you to tell us what weight of chloral was administered?"

"No."

"You cannot form any judgment?"

"No."

"And, of course, you don't know whether this amount of chloral would cause death?"

"That is not a matter that comes within my province."

"In the third jar there was no chloral?"

"No."

"Do you know where the contents of that jar came from?"

"From the abdominal cavity, I believe."

"Have you ever tested chloral in any other case of poisoning?"

"No. There have been no cases of intentional poisoning with chloral, so far as I have read on the subject."

"Then there has never been any analysis, and I may take it that this is the first case of the kind?"

"Yes."

"Chloral is also produced, is it not, by the action of chlorine on alcohol?"

"Yes; that is the way in which it is made. Chloral is a powder, which with the addition of a small quantity of water, forms a clear, colourless solution."

"Is chloroform formed from chloral in the stomach?"

"It is a disputed point."

"You are the only gentleman who has analysed the contents of the stomach of this poor man?"

"That is so."

"You have had no one to assist you?"

"No, my son was present, but he did not assist me."

McKeand concluded, "And the matter rests entirely with you."

Under re-examination by Hopwood, the witness was asked, "You say chloral poisoning has not been inquired into by this process. Are you speaking of any cases which you have read or heard of?"

"In cases where chloral is present, where a minute quantity exists in organic matter, it is only possible to get it by one of these kinds of processes."

"That is not the point. This is, you say, the first case in which an analysis has been made for a Court of Justice, but there have been many cases of poisoning?"

"That is so. They have not been analysed because where chloral has been taken either accidentally or otherwise, it has been known without the analyst having made these scientific tests."

"Are you convinced that there was chloral in the stomach?"

"I have not the slightest doubt about it."

Dr Julius Dreschfold, professor of pathology at Victoria University next stated, "I have made the case a study for the purpose of giving evidence. I have heard the evidence that has been given and the opinions of Drs Reynolds and Hampden-Barker and Mr Estcourt. I examined the heart, liver, and contents of the stomach, the kidneys, and other parts of the body of the deceased, and made a microscopic examination."

Hopwood asked, "Have you formed any idea of what was the immediate cause of death?"

The witness replied, "I have. The cause of death was syncope – syncope produced from the combined effects of chloral and alcohol upon a system already diseased by long, continued abuse of alcohol."

"Have you turned your attention to the question whether death would have proceeded, in your judgment, from the use of alcohol alone?"

"I have, and in my opinion death could not have proceeded from alcohol alone."

"Can you give your authority for saying death was not due to alcohol alone?"

"Alcohol may produce death in two ways. Either it is very sudden death from syncope or, what is very rare, death from syncope preceded by long, continued coma. In the first case the person taking it would suddenly fall down dead."

The Judge then inquired, "You mean by the word 'sudden' – instantaneous?"

"Yes. In the second case the coma might be long continued. A person having had a large dose of ardent spirits, such as a half pint or pint of whisky, might die suddenly. Death might also be caused by fatty degeneration of the heart or extensive hemorrhage of the brain. In the deceased I found incipient fatty degeneration of the heart and slight congestion of the brain, but no hemorrhage of the brain. If for an hour before death Mr Fletcher was drinking beer and sherry, that certainly excludes the notion that he died from an overdose of spirits. Seeing that the deceased had been walking about an hour before death there was certainly no coma. The fact that death occurred so soon after was incompatible with the theory of death by alcoholic poisoning, inasmuch as there was only partial insensibility not many minutes before death. It was a case of death by sudden syncope. There was also the circumstance that the deceased was described as having walked from the Three Arrows less than an hour before. That would not indicate alcoholic coma. The condition in which I found the body of the deceased was consistent with death by chloral."

Hopwood again, "Was there anything in the general condition of the body alone to account for death?"

"Not to account for death by natural causes," replied Dreschfold.

"If a dose of chloral was administered to the deceased at the Three Arrows, would his subsequent condition be consistent with chloral poisoning?"

"Certainly, of course depending on the quantity given. Drunkards could take a larger dose of chloral than sober men without hurt, but they could not do so when they were drunk. The two agents when together are more powerful."

"You have heard the evidence of the other medical gentlemen, do you agree with them?"

"I do."

"Is it a fact that chloral is rapidly absorbed in the system?"

"Yes, a few minutes after being taken."

"And does that make it difficult after death on examination to find a trace?"

"It depends how soon death takes place; also on the condition of the intestines."

"It is suggested that chloral might be present in some form naturally. Do you know anything of that sort."

"Certainly not."

"Have you made any experiment with chloral?"

"Yes, I have. Here is a bottle in which I placed ninety grains and dissolved it in water. I found it did not alter the colour of water nor the colour of beer into which I also placed some. Neither did it affect the taste on drinking it, but it did afterwards. Ninety grains are not a quantity that a medical man would give. After a little time there is a pungent taste experienced in the back of the throat.

Under cross-examination by McKeand, Dreschfold was asked, "If thirty grains had been put in Mr. Fletcher's beer, you would expect him to find a pungent taste?"

"A slightly pungent taste."

"And would that sensation at the back of the throat become stronger as he got to the bottom of the glass; would the chloral sink?"

"It is easily soluble, and would be easily diffused."

"If it took him twenty minutes to drink his beer, would not the pungency be coming on gradually?"

"Assuming that he was sipping, he would feel the pungency at each sip."

"Are the symptoms of chloral and alcoholic poisoning almost identical."

"Yes."

"Can you judge from the portions of the body you saw whether Mr Fletcher was of a temperate habit?"

"I should say not. He had a large liver. It was not a gin-drinker's liver, it was more a fatty liver. Syncope may be the result of alcoholic poisoning as well as chloral poisoning."

"In acute cases is it more likely to happen to a man who has no food in his stomach than to a man who has?"

"It would not make very much difference."

"Can you say positively that this man, Mr Fletcher, could not have died from alcoholic poisoning?"

"If I am to give my opinion…"

"Your opinion is that he died from the effects of chloral and alcohol combined. What I ask you is are you prepared to pledge your professional reputation that this man could not have died from alcoholic poisoning?"

"I should say it is highly improbable but yet possible."

His Lordship stated, "That is a scientific man's answer."

This closed the case for the prosecution and Hopwood in reviewing the evidence for the jury said, "The prisoner is young, and his youth might lead you down the line of sympathy, if your public duty would allow you to indulge in such feelings; but if he is the man the evidence proves, then he has shown himself to be abandoned to a wicked course of robbery and to be totally indifferent to the safety of human life. The evidence that has been adduced has been given with the strictest impartially. By the demeanour of the witness Phillips I believe that he was distilling truth drop by drop. The cross-examination by Mr McKeand amounted to two things. First, that the witness never saw what he said he saw. But have you any doubt that he did? What interest could he have in coming here and almost swear away a fellow creature's life? My learned friend, in cross-examination, next tried to make out that it was not chloral which was put into the beer, but something else, and by pressure he induced the witness to say that it was a yellow fluid. But let's imagine what would be the appearance of the substance through a bottle when held in contact with a glass of beer of a reddish colour. A white substance……..''

The Judge interrupted by saying, "A colourless substance – white is not a colour."

Hopwood continued, "A crystal fluid or a substance like water which was in juxtaposition with a glass of beer would reflect that colour and would present the impression of a yellow fluid. The circumstance also occurred in a bar-parlour in a strong gaslight, and therefore, when the witness said the liquid was of a yellowish colour, do you think he was giving anything more than his impression? Did it exclude the fact that it was chloral? I will now consider the evidence of the chemist, Mr Bromley, and I say in regard to him, that if ever there was a witness who recommended himself to a jury by his moderation and his conduct in the box it was Mr Bromley, and yet he identified the prisoner as the man who had stolen the chloral out of his shop. It proved that the prisoner had chloral in his possession, and what followed? The unfortunate gentleman, in a few minutes, was in a state of collapse, the chloral, according to the witness, having just previously been produced. The medical evidence left no doubt as to the cause of death, and I contend that the prisoner's intention was to hocus the unfortunate deceased, in order that he might, with deliberation, rob him of the valuables and money in his possession.

"That closes the case for the prosecution."

CHAPTER XIX

The Trial, Day Two, March 19th, The Verdict

McKeand then addressed the jury for the defence. "I appear before you not only as an advocate on behalf of a prisoner charged with a crime on the enormity of which we need not dwell, but as a man appealing to men for the life of a fellow creature. I cannot conceal either from you or from myself the anxiety this position entails upon me; because in defending a man for a charge of murder, and a charge of murder of this terrible kind, the law has placed upon me a terrible responsibility, but compared with that which devolves upon you, my duty is nothing. You have to say, once and for all, whether the man is to go back to freedom and liberty, or to go in the grey of an April morning to the scaffold to die. That is a terrible responsibility but, I am sure you will mete out to the man at the bar that fair and even-handed justice that is the proud boast of this great country.

"I will not be saying an untruth when I say that this is one of the most important cases tried for a great number of years. It is a matter of vital importance, not only

Image of the Trial Defence Lawyer, Mr McKeand, published in the
Liverpool Echo *Monday March 19th, 1889.*

to the prisoner, but to society at large, because if the story of the prosecution is true, it is a terrible thing to suppose that we have in our midst, and in great cities like Liverpool and Manchester, scoundrels going about armed with poisonous drugs, which they employ to rob and plunder drunken men, who in that condition fall easy victim to them. It is of the greatest importance, therefore, that in this particular instance you should be satisfied beyond a doubt, first that the young man administered chloral to Mr Fletcher, and, secondly that Mr Fletcher died in consequence of that administration.

"My learned friend, Mr Hopwood, has put the case fairly, and I agree with him when he said that the administration of a noxious drug with the intention of committing a felony is, in case death ensued, murder and nothing else. Although you might even be of the opinion that this young man did administer that chloral, I am sure not one of you is of the opinion that he ever contemplated for one moment the terrible and disastrous consequences which followed. But the question of intent is utterly immaterial. If the chloral was administered by him and caused death that was murder, and could not, by any construction of law, be reduced to manslaughter or any other form of crime. You must either find this man guilty of wilful murder or you must say that he is not guilty.

"There was nothing absolutely suspicious in the fact that Mr Fletcher and a young man of the prisoner's condition of life were together. The prosecution claim that the young man went with Mr Fletcher to the Three Arrows public house. According to the police evidence that house is usually very full, and if it had been in the prisoner's mind to drug him, do you suppose for one moment that he would choose the Three Arrows? Here was a large room where he might have expected to have met, it does not matter how many, a large number of persons, and that being so what opportunity would he have to have drugged Mr Fletcher, if all those persons were there? There are, as some of you might know, hundreds of public houses, quiet little places, where had he been so minded, he could have taken Mr Fletcher, and perpetrated this outrage upon him without the chance of being detected, and without the chance of being seen by a soul, except the person who might probably have served him with the beer. When they went away from the Three Arrows in a cab they went by direction of the prisoner along some of the busiest streets in Manchester, and it seems incredible that if the prisoner intended to rob Mr Fletcher, he should have taken this route. The prosecution, have suggested that the address, 43, Stretford Road, which the prisoner gave was a 'blind,' but the fact is that 43, Stretford Road is a corner house in the neighbourhood of certain houses – I will not suggest more.

"In reference to the occurrences in the Three Arrows public house, it is a very great misfortune in a case like this, when a man charged with the offence of murder, that he should have sprung upon him, at the eleventh hour, evidence which if you believe it, namely that of Mr Phillips, was absolutely conclusive against the prisoner. If you believe Phillips, there is the end to my case, so far as the theory

I suggested went. If notice had been given to the defence that he was going to be called, it would have given me the opportunity of inquiring about his reputation and ascertaining how long he was at the Three Arrows. The prosecution, however, were quite within their rights."

His Lordship said, "I understood notice had been given."

McKeand responded, "Certainly I had some notice but it was at the eleventh hour. It was on Friday night and the trial commenced Monday morning. Also, Inspector Caminada behaved poorly by putting detailed questions to Phillips instead of merely asking him, 'What is your evidence?' And how did Mr. Phillips explain his conduct? He gave two reasons. One was that he did not want to lose his situation, and the other was incredible – he did not come forward, he said, because he did not consider his evidence material. Phillips was sitting in a corner, and he said he deliberately saw the prisoner produce a bottle. Does it not strike you as being rather odd that he should have held up the glass to the light? While he was doing all this there were five other people who were sitting opposite to the prisoner. Not one of those persons was called to give evidence. You might be perfectly certain that Mr Caminada, who prides himself upon being the most experienced detective in the North of England, would have endeavoured to find out those persons and everything about them, and that being so I am entitled to assume that the evidence of those five persons, when given, would have been absolutely nil.

"You were asked by the prosecution what motive Phillips would have had in coming here practically to swear away the life of a fellow creature. But the answer was given by the witness himself, that he did not consider his evidence material. But he now knows how terribly material it was. It often happens that persons led away by excitement say they saw things which they did not see, but having made statements they do not like to contradict, they believe that their statements are not material. With the exception of the witness Mr Bromley, no one traced chloral to the possession of the prisoner, and it is not beyond the range of possibility that Mr. Bromley might be mistaken as to the identity of the thief who entered his shop. The light was bad at the time, Mr Bromley is an elderly man, and he only saw the man who stole the chloral for a half moment.

"Assuming for the purpose of argument that the prisoner did not administer chloral, what was more natural, if he was a thief, as the prosecution suggested he was, than that he, seeing Mr Fletcher in the cab in a condition more or less comatose from drink, should seize the opportunity of relieving him of his watch and guard and getting away? Gentlemen, do you think that the prisoner believed Mr. Fletcher was going to die? Did he act immediately after he left the cab like a man who had committed a terrible crime? No, he at once went and destroyed all chance of losing his identity by exhibiting himself in the York Minster and on the box of a cab. Action of that kind might be foolish, but it was not the set of a man who had just committed a diabolical crime. When Parton was arrested he told Caminada that he had seven or eight witnesses who would prove he was not with Mr Fletcher on the 26th of February, but this was untrue. As many men do when they are arrested he told a deliberate lie, but your minds should not be prejudiced against him on that account.

"Turning to the medical evidence, I would like to ask what after all did it amount to? Chloral poisoning is a matter of deep research, and I have done all I could with my limited knowledge to bring forward all the facts which ought to have been brought forward to establish the theory. I suggest to you that Mr Fletcher died from alcoholic and not from chloral poisoning, or that the actual cause of death the medical evidence has left so much in doubt that you are entitled to give the benefit of that doubt to the prisoner. On suspicion no man must be convicted.

"In considering your verdict, you ought to remember that there are made against the prisoner other grave and terrible charges, which have been indicated, and if the man is acquitted of murder he will not go from the dock scot-free. Had Mr Fletcher been a man of respectable habits as far as the consumption of alcohol was concerned my observations in regard to the doubt as to his death would not be necessary, but Mr Fletcher had a gin drinker's liver, partial fatty degeneration of the heart, partial congestion of the lungs and all his organs more or less affected by drink. It was because he was in that condition that the abuse of alcohol would produce syncope and syncope death. The medical evidence is, of course, always more or less theoretical, and in this instance, had no trace of chloral been found in the body, Dr Hampden-Barker would have been satisfied to have certified that the man died from alcoholic poisoning. So there is a doubt. Mr Estcourt had put the contents of the stomach to three tests and the same result was arrived at. He said there were traces of chloroform in the stomach, the presence of which showed that chloral had been taken. I do not wish to make any suggestions against Mr Estcourt's experience, but Mr Estcourt is only a man, and he could make mistakes like doctors or anyone else. Therefore you ought to receive his evidence to a certain extent with a great deal of care and caution, having regard to the fact that this was the first case of the kind that has come under his notice, and that being so it would not be right to rely too strongly upon mere theories of medical men. Theories might, no doubt, be strong sometimes, especially when men who have vast experience show that those theories were corroborated over and over again. But where you have a theory for the first time, would it be right in a question of life and death, to rely too implicitly upon it?

"The sole matter before you is, did this young man administer the chloral and was chloral the cause of death? Unless you can answer those questions in the affirmative, and if there is any reasonable doubt which can be entertained by reasonable men, the young man at the bar is entitled to leave the dock free from the terrible charge hanging over him. This case has been called the mystery of a four-wheeled cab, and it had been rightly called, because from first to last it has been enveloped in perfect clouds of mystery and doubt, which you have today been asked to unravel. I ask you to say, and to tell the public by your verdict, that you have swept and dashed on one side all the clouds of mystery and doubt in which Mr Fletcher's death was involved, and that you have sent the prisoner forth once again and for ever, as this terrible charge is concerned, to liberty and life."

At this point McKeand concluded his closing remarks.

The Judge, Mr Justice Charles, then proceeded to sum up the case at 12:20. He addressed the jury saying, "The question you have to consider is one of the gravest importance to the public, and of the very last importance to the prisoner. The prisoner stands on trial for his life. He is indicted for the willful murder, with malice aforethought, of Mr John Fletcher. I am bound to state at once that if the prosecution has made out to your satisfaction that the prisoner at the bar did administer a stupefying drug to Mr Fletcher with the intention of robbing him and, if, further, the effect of the administration of the stupefying drug, was to kill Mr Fletcher or materially contribute to his death, then the prisoner is guilty beyond all doubt of wilful murder. Volumes have been written upon the meaning of the words 'malice aforethought,' and in the present case I need not trouble you with any lengthy remarks upon it. But, if one thing is clearer than another it is this; that if one person administered a stupefying drug to another with the intention of robbing him, and death ensued on administration of the drug, then the person who administered it is guilty of wilful murder. It is not disputed that if this young man did administer that drug, and, if that drug caused the death of Mr. Fletcher, then you must find the prisoner guilty of wilful murder. I must tell you that you must not concern yourself with the consequences of that verdict. It might be that it is a sad thing to pronounce a verdict of guilty against a young man like the prisoner, but you must not shrink from performing your duty if you are of the opinion that guilt has been brought home to him. If you have any doubt as to whether the prisoner administered chloral, or, you have any doubt whether chloral caused the death of John Fletcher; if you can see your way as reasonable men to any doubt upon the question, the prosecution, I know, will be glad you should give the prisoner the benefit of it. The duty now passes from the bar to you. It has been admirably discharged at the bar.

"The prosecution has laid before you with such perfect fairness as one would expect from the learned Recorder of Liverpool, and the defence has been laid before you with admiral judgment. Now comes your duty and your responsibility. You have to consider whether this young man administered a stupefying drug to Mr Fletcher with intent to rob him, and whether the drug so administered killed him or materially contributed to his death. The deceased, Mr Fletcher, was unhappily, too fond of drink, although it was far from being suggested that he was a drunkard. At one time it seemed likely you would have a very grave and embarrassing question to consider, and that was whether the young man who got into the cab at twenty minutes to seven o'clock on Tuesday the 26th of February, was or was not, the prisoner at the bar; but there are limits to all things, and the evidence produced on the part of the prosecution of witness after witness soon convinced Mr McKeand that it was useless to struggle against the identity of the young man. A young man who was seen to get into this cab with Mr. Fletcher at twenty minutes to seven, at twenty five minutes past seven was seen exhibiting property – although we are not now trying the question of property – which had no doubt been stolen from Mr Fletcher – at the York Minster public house."

His Lordship then proceeded to review the medical evidence. "The important and critical part of the case is the medical evidence. Did Mr Fletcher die of alcoholic poisoning alone, or did he die of chloral poisoning or of a combination of alcohol and chloral. If your minds are left in doubt, any reasonable doubt that a body of intelligent men could entertain, then Mr McKeand is right and you ought to acquit the prisoner. But after all, probabilities are what you have to act upon, and if you would allow me to say so, it would never do to indulge in speculations about possibilities when the evidence given in the case pointed to a highly probable and almost certain solution. There is an unanimity of opinion as to the result of the *post-mortem* examination. If Mr Fletcher died of alcohol poisoning alone you are justified in acquitting the prisoner, but if you think he died of chloral poisoning, and that the prisoner administered the chloral, then you certainly ought to convict him. If that unfortunate man died from the combination of alcohol with chloral, and the chloral was administered by the prisoner then, however painful might be your duty, it is your duty to find the prisoner guilty."

Image of Charles Parton published in the Liverpool Echo *Monday March 18th, 1889.*

THE TRIAL, DAY TWO, MARCH 19TH, THE VERDICT

In closing his observations his Lordship said to the jury, "If you are of the opinion that the young man at the bar administered the drug with the intention of committing a felony, it does not matter whether he meant to kill or not, he is guilty. It has been proven that a week previous, the prisoner possessed himself of some chloral, and therefore, you have the facts, unless Mr Bromley was mistaken, that the prisoner had chloral, that he was in the Three Arrows, and that he there administered the drug to Mr Fletcher.

"If the death of the deceased followed from the administration of a drug; if chloral was found in the man's body, and if the doctors told you that, to the best of their judgment, the death of the man was due to chloral acting upon the brain of a man accustomed to drinking; if again the symptoms of chronic alcoholic poisoning are wanting and if the symptoms of sudden alcoholic poisoning are also wanting; what are you to say? You must find the prisoner guilty. If, however, you find or come to the conclusion, that there really exists a doubt, which reasonable men might entertain as to the cause of this man's death, by all means you may say so, and acquit the prisoner; but if, as twelve reasonable men, having listened to the evidence of the doctors and the analyst, and to the facts of the case affecting the prisoner in connection with the administration of the drug, you come to the conclusion that the prisoner's was the hand that administered the drug, and that the administration of the drug materially contributed to the death of Mr Fletcher then, however sad and grave your task might be, you must come to the conclusion that the prisoner is guilty."

The jury retired to consider their verdict at half-past one. Throughout the day the prisoner wore the same air of calmness that had characterized his demeanour on Monday, but as the case drew to a close he became evidently nervous and despondent. After an absence of about twenty minutes the jury again entered the box. In answer to the Clerk of the Crown, the Foreman said they found the prisoner guilty of murder. They accompanied their verdict with a strong recommendation to mercy on account of his youth.

The Clerk of the Assizes then asked Parton the usual question, "Do you have anything to say why sentence of death should not be passed upon you?" Parton, who was leaning over the front of the dock betraying little emotion, though the muscles of the lower half of his face were twitching as though he was setting his teeth, shook his head and in a faint voice replied, "No."

The Judge, having put on the black cap, in passing sentence addressed the prisoner, "Charles Parton, the jury has found you guilty of the crime of willful murder. I feel bound to say that upon the evidence offered in this court they could have come to no other conclusion. They are of the opinion that you administered a drug to Mr John Fletcher, and that Mr Fletcher died from the administration of that drug. Therefore, they have found you guilty as they were bound to find you guilty. I don't desire by any words of mine to aggravate the terrible position in which you are placed. It is my solemn duty to tell you that you must prepare to die. You have forfeited your life to the law. I don't desire to say anything more except to beg you, as earnestly as I can, to repent of the crime of which you have been convicted. Do not build upon the recommendation which the jury have added to their verdict. I know not what will be the result of that recommendation."

His Lordship then pronounced sentence of death. "Charles Parton, the sentence of the law is that you to be taken from hence to the place from whence you came, and thence to the place of execution, and that you be hanged by the neck until you are dead, and that your body be afterward buried within the precincts of the prison in which you shall be confined after your conviction. And may the Lord have mercy upon your soul. Amen."

The convict, who during his Lordship's observations had convulsively clutched the front rail of the dock, showed no other outward sign of emotion. He stepped quickly down into the cells below the court, closely attended by the warders.

PART FOUR
ANALYSIS OF THE CASE

CHAPTER XX

The Press Commentaries

After the verdict of the trial much press comment was published the following day. Typical excerpts are included here.

The *Manchester Courier* reported that, "Great credit is due to the Chief Constable of Manchester and to his excellent lieutenant, Chief Detective Inspector Caminada, for the thoroughness with which they had succeeded in unravelling what, at the time, was regarded as a serious outrage. It would have been a sad thing if the murderer had escaped detection. The crime was of so secret and subtle a character that failure on the part of the police would have been followed by more or less alarm among the inhabitants, and the exceedingly clever manner in which the various links in the chain of evidence which brought the offence home to Parton have been produced will have the efficacy not only of restoring confidence, but of assuring the public that the guilt of the culprit has been incontestably established. The whole business – the crime, the capture, the trial and the sentence of death – has been accomplished in about three weeks. The miserable culprit was a prominent figure amongst 'fast' young men. He had acquired some skill as a boxer; and the loose habits that skill induced, and the disreputable company into which it brought him, blunted his moral nature and made him a thief. Such people can be spared, and it is to be regretted that they cannot be got rid of until they have inflicted irreparable mischief upon society. However, it is satisfactory to know that what has been called the 'Manchester Cab Mystery' has been solved."

The London *Daily Telegraph* said, "In the case of the so-called 'Manchester Cab Mystery,' the old adage 'Murder will out,' of late so frequently controverted by the recurrent impunity of undetected assassins, has been triumphantly verified. The knowledge that atrocious criminals – such as the perpetrator of the Whitechapel butcheries, for instance – have succeeded in evading discovery for many months and are still at liberty (in all probability rubbing shoulders daily with well-conducted and law-abiding persons), is heavily fraught with mortification to the people of a civilised country.

"Experience has repeatedly proved within the last few years that the mechanism at the disposal of our Home Office is not always adequate to the fulfillment of the objects it has been specially organized to achieve. That it should show itself equal to its task in bringing the murderer of Mr John Fletcher to trial with laudable promptitude is really a subject for self-congratulation. The crime to which the unfortunate Manchester gentleman fell victim presented more than one feature of peculiar vileness. It was the result of a deeply-laid scheme, carefully thought out and put into execution with cold-blooded mercilessness, whilst its motive was a despicably base one. Mr Fletcher was done to death in order that his slayer might gain possession of his gold watch and chain and the handful of loose money which a man in easy circumstances may, as a rule, be assumed to carry about in his waistcoat and trouser pockets. Nothing transpired in the course of the evidence adduced at the trial of Charles Parton to indicate that this precocious miscreant – a mere stripling of eighteen – entertained any animosity towards the kindly, jovial gentleman whom he deliberately murdered and robbed.

"Parton's crime had been so ingeniously planned, and, on the whole, was so cleverly executed, that but for two circumstances – one attributable to his own imprudence, and the other purely accidental – it might have escaped detection, and he himself might have got off scot free. Mr Fletcher, it appears, was sufficiently given to indulgence in intoxicating liquors to justify the assumption that he had died of alcoholic poisoning, the result of habitual intemperance. As a matter of fact, that was the view taken of the cause of death by the house surgeon of the Manchester Infirmary, Dr Hampden-Barker, who first examined his body when it was brought to that institution. Dr Reynolds, another member of the Infirmary medical staff, who took part in the *post-mortem* examination, stated that the deceased was a bullnecked man, who had undoubtedly consumed a vast amount of ardent spirits, and whose liver was that of an habitual gin drinker 'in an early stage.' Neither he nor his colleague, Dr Hampden-Barker, would swear that Mr Fletcher had not died from alcoholic poisoning. Thus it might have been impossible for the prosecution to prove Parton's guilt despite his suspicious behaviour on the night of the murder – when he sported the spoils of his victim in a public house – had not the two circumstances above referred to been brought home to him with fatal directness. The first was the theft of a bottle of chloral from a chemist's shop in Liverpool, just a week before the murder.

"Possibly the fact that Parton was in possession of a pound of chloral, obtained by nefarious means, at the time when he persuaded Mr Fletcher to drink and ride in a cab with him, might have been regarded from the strictly legal point of view merely a piece of strong presumptive evidence in his disfavour, considered in conjunction with other criminal matters that came to light in the course of the trial. All doubt as to his culpability, however, was removed by the testimony of a witness who had held aloof from the magisterial investigations preceding Parton's committal on the capital charge, but who came forward to swear that he had seen the prisoner furtively pour the contents of a phial into one of the two glasses of beer with which Mr Fletcher and Parton were supplied at the Three Arrows public house. His evidence practically cleared up the 'Manchester Cab Mystery,' and sealed the fate of Parton."

The *Liverpool Courier* reported that, "What it has been the custom to call the 'Manchester Cab Mystery' is now solved. We do not know what may be the effect of the strong recommendation to mercy on account of the youth of the convict, nor shall we express an opinion on the subject. But it will be admitted that this youth's plan of plunder was as diabolically ingenious as any that could have been devised by the oldest and most hardened criminal. It speaks, indeed, to a precociousness in fiendish arts, thoroughly in keeping with the extraordinary callousness which enabled this abnormal refinement of Bill Sykes to go below and heartily discuss savoury dinner – being the last that could be provided by his friends – while the jury were deliberating as to his doom. There are not many venerables in the ranks of crime who in the circumstances would have been equal to such a performance. We are not surprised that the ladies in court sobbed when the last dread sentence of the law was passed upon this stripling culprit. It was none the less evident that their emotion was entirely thrown away upon the prisoner, who to the last moment was the cool, self-possessed, callous desperado which his acts, in spite of his years, had proclaimed him to be."

The *Manchester Guardian* said that, "The Manchester 'cab mystery' is a mystery no longer. It has been proved to the satisfaction of the judge and jury at the Liverpool Assizes, and also, there can be little doubt, to the world at large, that Mr John Fletcher died from the effects of a drug administered to him by the young man Parton with the object of facilitating a robbery which was then contemplated. The case has excited an enormous amount of public interest; and not unnaturally so, for the crime of which Parton was accused was one of a peculiarly treacherous character, and one, moreover, so easily committed that the detection and conviction of the criminal was felt to be a matter of the first importance. Thanks to the acuteness of the Manchester detective force, the desired result has been obtained; and within a few days of the actual commission of the crime the murderer has been tried and condemned. The murder of Mr Fletcher has riveted public attention to a degree quite as engrossing as that which excited the crimes of Palmer and Dove thirty years ago. In each case the agent employed by the assassin was entirely new in the annals of our jurisprudence. Palmer and Dove used strychnine, a drug whose peculiar qualities were then not widely known; Parton used chloral, a drug which in beneficent hands is used for the alleviation of pain, but which given in excess destroys life as certainly as the more active agent. The young man who was condemned yesterday seems to have acquired some knowledge of the stupefying effect of chloral from seeing it administered to his own father; and there is every reason to believe that he resolved to employ it in order to facilitate robbery, careless whether or not he administered a fatal dose. In this case, it is satisfactory to observe that science, which had supplied the agent by which the crime was committed, also furnished justice with the means of bringing the assassin to his richly deserved punishment. The men of science who were examined during the trial were able to point with unerring certainty to the cause of death. The traces were slight, but convincing; and it is well for the public safety that persons who might be disposed to imitate Parton's method should know that this latest form of secret poisoning is just as liable to detection as were the commoner forms of murder by the administration of strychnine or other deadly ingredients. The jury recommended the convict to mercy on account of his youth; but it is notorious that the robbery which has had such awful consequences was not the first, nor the second, in which he had employed the same subtle agent; and that being so, it is obvious that the probabilities are in favour of the sentence being carried out."

Later in the month, the *Illustrated Police News* of March 30th commented, "We are always glad when we can conscientiously say a good word for the police. Solely owing to the vigilance of the constabulary the Manchester cab mystery has been satisfactorily solved. Everything has been cleared up, and there is no longer any mystification. Charles Parton has within three weeks been tried and found guilty, and now awaits execution. He is a mere stripling – eighteen – and his youth induced the jury at the assizes to recommend him to mercy. Whether the sentence is carried out or not, this crime, so clearly brought home to him, was of the most despicable and heinous character, happily of rare occurrence. Mr John Fletcher, a Manchester gentleman, was the victim of this precocious scoundrel, who for the possession of a gold watch and chain and the loose money which Mr Fletcher might perchance have on his person, conceived the idea of poisoning him. On the evening of February 26th Fletcher and Parton were at the Three Arrows, Deansgate, drinking together, and Parton was distinctly seen to empty a small bottle, containing a yellowish liquid, into one of the glasses. Mr Fletcher, who was talking at the time, failed to perceive the trick, and the person who did see it considered that a dose of medicine was simply being put into the drink. Driven off in a cab, Mr Fletcher, who had drunk the fatal dose – for the drink contained chloral stolen by Parton from the shop of a chemist at Liverpool – was robbed and afterwards found next to dead. Mr. Fletcher died soon afterwards, the victim of a diabolical, well-laid scheme to murder him. The defence set up, that death was attributable to alcoholic poisoning, was worthy of those ardent teetotalers who set down anything and everything that is bad to the indulgence in drink. The Public Analyst found traces of chloral in the body of Fletcher, and that settled the matter. The police are to be congratulated upon the solution of this mystery. To be foully murdered as was Mr Fletcher, to have a deadly dose administered in a glass of beer by a seeming friend, and a criminal to go at large undetected, might well be regarded as a horror too dreadful to contemplate. But the old adage that 'murder will out' has in this case of a 'Mystery of a Hansom Cab' at Manchester been once more verified."

In another part of the same edition of the *Illustrated Police News* it was reported that, "Parton, the hero of the Manchester cab mystery, is not the sort of man who allows himself to be done out of his dinner. When the jury had retired to consider their verdict he preferred a mild request for leave to descend to the lower regions and support exhausted nature with a little light refreshment. Leave was accordingly granted, and Parton retired below and had a most satisfactory 'feed.' Certainly the condemned murderer is in his generation wise. Parton's friends had got him a sumptuous dinner ready, but if he had waited until after the sentence had made him a convicted felon he would have had to chew dainties, and put up with strict prison fare."

CHAPTER XXI

The Medical Debate

Despite the jury reaching their verdict in twenty minutes, presumably, largely based on the identification of the prisoner and the medical evidence, and regardless of Mr Justice Charles' confidence in the medical men, a lively debate ensued on the quality of the medical evidence. The debate took place through letters to the *British Medical Journal*. Relevant portions of the letters are presented below.

Dr Gumpert, a local physician of Manchester, wrote to the *British Medical Journal* and the following letter was published in the 30th March, 1889, edition. "Sir – The verdict given by the jury who sat at Liverpool last week to try Charles Parton for wilful murder will not have astonished many medical men – not even those who, like myself, consider it utterly wrong. Whilst I do not blame any one person engaged in the case, it is the atrocious system under which criminal prosecutions of this kind are managed in England, at whose door I lay the charge that a man has been condemned for a murder which probably was not committed.

"I maintain that the death of Mr Fletcher was most probably not caused by a dose of chloral hydrate, and this might have been made quite evident to the prosecution if we had the system of trying to find out the truth in such cases as is customary in Continental States. I admit that a quantity of chloral was administered in a glass of beer to the deceased with the felonious intent of robbing him, and that, if death was the consequence of this act, it was wilful murder according to English law. The all important question, therefore, is: Was that dose sufficient to have a fatal effect, even in the case of a person suffering from chronic alcoholism and fatty degeneration of the heart?

"Now, according to the evidence of the analyst, only traces of chloral could be found in the contents of the stomach. If only 20 or 30 grains were taken about an hour before death in half a pint of beer – and a not inconsiderable quantity of beer is found in the stomach – I maintain that some grains of chloral could be found, and not only traces. From the time of Mr Fletcher's death, on the evening of February 26th, to the afternoon of March 19th, when sentence of death was passed on Charles Parton, not quite three weeks have elapsed, the time it would take – at least on the Continent – to make a thorough chemical analysis, and to draw up a medical report on the symptoms exhibited by the deceased, on the *post-mortem* examination, and on the result of the chemical analysis. Both the medical and chemical reports, accompanied by protocols stating most minutely and with almost pedantic accuracy everything that was done and how it was done during these respective investigations, are submitted for approval or otherwise to a council of specially-appointed medical men well versed in forensic medicine.

"The analyst is not chosen haphazard – say by a man like our clever Manchester detective, for whose skill and abilities in his particular sphere I have the greatest respect – but by the authorities, with the assistance of men well able to form an opinion of the requisite qualifications. If the same analyst who gave evidence in this case examines some adulterated milk with the view of a prosecution, his evidence would not be received in court unless, if the defendant should wish, a sample of the same milk had been retained for analysis by an expert to be chosen by the defendant, and another sample submitted to the authorities at Somerset House, if in case of a discrepancy this should be found advisable. But then it is a question of fining perhaps a milk dealer £10, and there are many people under the impression that property is held much more sacred than human life. Anybody who is in the habit of reading the cases tried under the Adulteration of Food and Drugs Act must have seen that the prosecution founded on the evidence of public analysts, many of them good and capable men, frequently fails owing to the evidence given for the defence by equally good, and sometimes better men. The medical witnesses for the prosecution – there were no skilled witnesses for the defence owing to the want of funds, the brief being only put in counsel's hand ten minutes after the case had commenced – seem to have entirely ignored the statement that only traces of chloral could be detected in the stomach. The immediate cause of Mr. Fletcher's death was syncope. The cases of death from syncope after large doses of chloral-hydrate (80-grain and more) are very rare, and were invariably accompanied by acute oedema of the lungs, which seems to have been absent in this case. I am etc., E. Gumpert M.D., Manchester, March 25th."

Dr Julius Dreschfold, professor of pathology at Victoria University responded to Dr Gumpert's letter in the same publication. His letter was published in the April 6th edition. "Sir, Though I disagree with Dr Gumpert as to the cause of Mr. Fletcher's death, yet I entirely endorse his condemnation of our present mode of procedure in criminal investigations. Not only should the necropsies and chemical investigations be conducted by experts, but in difficult and obscure cases a higher council of experts might well be appealed to for the guidance of the judge and jury. In this special case, however, the chain of evidence as to the administration of chloral was so complete that from it, from the symptoms observed during life, and from the *post-mortem* appearances, the medical witnesses could arrive at no other conclusion than that chloral was instrumental in causing the death of Mr Fletcher.

"Dr Gumpert admits that chloral was administered to the deceased, but lays great stress on the fact that traces only were found after death. How it was that the chemical analysis showed the presence of traces only I must leave the analyst to explain, but even if, as Dr Gumpert expected, some grains of that drug had been detected and separated, such a discovery would not have helped the medical evidence much, for no conclusions could thence be drawn as to the actual quantity administered, nor would it have been possible to tell whether the dose given was a likely fatal dose, as we know that in some cases thirty grains, in others a much larger quantity, proved fatal.

"The administration of chloral being once admitted, a surer and more reliable guide was found in the symptoms succeeding the administration, in the mode of death, and in the *post-mortem* appearances. On these points the evidence appears conclusive enough. A few minutes after the administration of chloral the deceased was rendered so insensible that he allowed himself to be robbed of his watch, chain, and money without a struggle. The insensibility deepened, but even fifteen minutes before death there was no coma, as he could readily be roused.

"The *post-mortem* appearances showed all those conditions seen in syncope from chloral; to wit, a fluid state of the blood, congestion of the lungs, and slight congestion of the membranes of the brain. On this subject, Dr Gumpert was misinformed. The necropsy report states that congestion of the lungs was present, and I need scarcely point out that oedema of the lungs is only a sequence of congestion. Dr Gumpert will further find from the published records of fatal cases of chloral poisoning that death from syncope is by no means unusual.

"If syncope was not caused by chloral, what was it due to? Dr Gumpert leaves the question unanswered; and I can only surmise that he supposes that we had here one of those rare cases of sudden death from syncope to which Mr Fletcher, from the condition of his heart and his liver, was perhaps more liable; and this happened, by a strange coincidence, at the very time that he had been given a dose of chloral. Such an assumption is not only very improbable, but, if maintained, might do an incalculable amount of harm, for the same plea might be set up in all cases of criminal deaths where the victim had taken some spirituous liquor shortly before death, and where the necropsy revealed fatty degeneration of the heart and liver – a combination of factors which surely is often found to exist.

"The question for the medical witnesses to answer was: Had chloral any share in causing death in this particular case? They were not asked to state what proportionate share it had, and to this question only one answer could be given. If, in consequence of that answer, the prisoner was found guilty of murder, and if Dr. Gumpert does not agree to that verdict, then he ought to blame the law, and not the medical witnesses. I am, etc., J. Dreschfold M.D., Manchester, April 1st."

Dr Ernest Reynolds, Resident Medical Officer, Manchester Royal Infirmary also responded to Dr Gumpert's letter and his letter was likewise published in the April 6th edition of the *British Medical Journal*. "Sir – In the Journal of March 30th there appears a letter from Dr Gumpert relating to the cause of death of Mr John Fletcher. In this letter there are made distinct charges of unjust judicial proceedings, of incompetent analysis, and of carelessness or ignorance of the medical witnesses: 'the medical witnesses for the prosecution seemed to have entirely ignored the statement that only traces of chloral could be detected in the stomach.' Concerning English law and chemical analysis I have now nothing whatever to say; but as the one who made the *post-mortem* examination and gave much of the medical evidence I feel bound to defend myself against the serious charges made by Dr Gumpert. In as much as I am at present preparing this interesting and important case for publication, I shall not now go more fully into the pros and cons of the matter, but can assure Dr Gumpert that the very greatest care and circumspection were used, as I was fully alive to the gravity of the charge made against Charles Parton.

"Secondly, I most strongly object to being called 'a medical witness for the prosecution.' A practitioner ordered to make a *post-mortem* examination by a coroner gives his evidence, first, on matters of fact, and, secondly, gives his opinion to the best of his professional ability, and, if he is an honest man, is absolutely unbiased either towards the prosecution or the prisoner.

"One suggested inference in your correspondent's letter I should like to correct at once: this is, that the analyst was chosen by 'our clever Manchester detective.' This is absolutely erroneous. The analyst was chosen by the proper authority, the City Coroner, and the analyst chosen was Mr Charles Estcourt, the analyst for the city of Manchester.

"Finally, if you will allow me to trespass further, I should like to remark that Mr Fletcher was undoubtedly dead when brought to the Manchester Royal Infirmary. Dr Gumpert maintains that he did not die of chloral, but entirely omits to suggest what he did die of. If Dr Gumpert will make a suggestion as to the cause of death, I will undertake to show the extreme improbability of any other cause but that of chloral. I am, etc., Ernest Reynolds, M.D., Manchester, April 2nd."

Fletcher was taken to the Infirmary in Piccadilly after PC Jakeman assessed the seriousness of his condition.

Dr Gumpert then followed with a second letter, responding to the letters of Drs Dreschfold and Reynolds, published in the April 13th edition. "Sir – I have read with the greatest satisfaction that Dr Dreschfold 'entirely endorses my condemnation of our present mode of procedure in criminal investigations,' and I trust that now, when the ball has been set rolling, others, more capable and influential than myself, will take up the matter, and will succeed in reconstructing that part of our present system which is antiquated and thoroughly bad. That Dr Reynolds, in making the *post-mortem* examination and in giving his evidence, used the very greatest care and circumspection, goes without saying.

"Neither of your correspondents argues the cardinal point on which my whole argument hinges, namely, the result of the chemical analysis being incompatible, in my opinion, with the assumption of the medical witnesses that a quantity of chloral had been administered to Mr Fletcher, large enough to have been instrumental in causing death. But I am truly thankful to Dr Dreschfold for the remark, 'How it was that the chemical analysis showed the presence of traces only, I must leave the analyst to explain.' Could anything, except the positive admission, show more clearly that Dr Dreschfold, at least, does think that larger quantities than mere traces were contained in the stomach, and that the analyst ought to have found them. Seeing that the analyst did not assist him, he ignored it entirely; and from the chain of evidence as to the administration of chloral, 'from the symptoms observed during life, and from the *post-mortem* appearances, the medical witnesses could arrive at no other conclusion than that chloral was instrumental in causing the death of Mr Fletcher.' But surely this is rather putting the cart before the horse, as I must strongly insist that we take the analyst, who was chosen by the prosecution, quite seriously. It is not admissible that in the tragedy, which has just been unrolled before our eyes, a most important part is treated as a farce. Unless my information is entirely at fault, all the medical witnesses admitted distinctly the possibility that chloral might *not* have been the cause of death in this case. Therefore, all the reasoning in the world as to its improbability is of no use whatsoever as soon as it can be proved that the quantity of chloral cannot possibly have been sufficiently large to have caused death under any circumstances. And this, I maintain, can be done, treating, of course, the analysis made as thoroughly reliable. Dr Dreschfold is quite mistaken when he thinks that I expected that some grains of that drug could have been detected and separated. I expected nothing either one way or another, but calmly waited for the result of the analysis, and on the result of that analysis I entirely, and without hesitation, have based my argument. What I really did say was, that, if only twenty or thirty grains had been taken, some grains of chloral could have been found, and not only traces.

"From the moment it was discovered that Mr Fletcher had been robbed there was chloral in the air, which became so stifling when evidence was given that the man suspected had drugged two other victims and had stolen a pound of chloral, that it affected the brain of the entire community, of the defence as well as the prosecution, and that, when the accused was tried for the murder of Mr Fletcher before three weeks had elapsed, he was, as a matter of course, found guilty by the jury.

"If I did not state before what, in my opinion, caused this fatal syncope, it was no doubt due to my thinking it quite irrelevant as long as I could bring independent proof that it was not due to chloral poisoning; but since your correspondents express a wish that I should give my opinion on this point, I willingly do so.

"A man on the wrong side of forty-five, suffering from chronic alcoholism, consumes on the afternoon of February 26th, between the hours of 12.45 and 6.40, a considerable quantity of alcohol, which must dangerously stimulate his weak heart to increased and irregular action. After standing for some time in the chilly air of a February evening, he enters the much warmer air of a tavern, where he partakes of a glass of beer, in which he finds the proverbial straw that breaks the camel's back. He stays for fifteen to twenty minutes, and after having entered a cab, accompanied by a young fellow, he gets, by the cumulative action of the alcohol consumed during the last six hours, rapidly into such a state of stupor that he allows himself to be robbed of his valuables. Being seen by the cabman about 7.15, immediately after his highly interesting companion has decamped, he is 'found in a stupid intoxicated condition,' telling the cabman, when he makes attempts at rousing him, 'to go away and leave him alone.' He is driven by a roundabout way to the Infirmary, and on the point of his arriving there he is heard to make a slight noise, apparently 'in his throat.' When taken out of the cab he is found to be dead.

"And what was to the best of my belief and knowledge the cause of his death? Primary, syncope; secondary (1), fatty de-generation of the heart, (2) chronic alcoholism, (3) acute alcoholic poisoning (one hour). I am etc., E. Gumpert, M.D., Manchester, April 9th."

CHAPTER XXII

Dr Ernest Reynolds' Medical Opinion

Dr. Ernest Reynolds mentioned in his letter of April 2nd to the *British Medical Journal* that he intended to publish his medical opinion of the case. His article entitled, "'The Manchester Murder'; Homicidal Chloral Poisoning, With Its Medico-legal Relations," appeared in the August 3rd edition of the *British Medical Journal*. Excerpts from the article follow.

"The so-called 'Manchester Cab Mystery' being, so far as I know, the first case on record of homicidal chloral poisoning, a detailed account may be of some interest. In addition, I have ventured to add a few remarks on chloral poisoning in its medico-legal relations.

"John Fletcher was initially examined by Dr J. H. Hampden-Barker, M.B. (Vict.), the house-physician, who found him quite pale, death evidently having been immediately due to syncope. There was no smell of chloroform or prussic acid, and the breath expressed from the lungs gave no reaction with silver nitrate, but smelt strongly of alcohol. I made the *post-mortem* examination at 3 P.M. on Wednesday, February 27th (weather very cold), assisted by Dr Hampden-Barker. The body was that of a heavy man, weighing about 15 stones, and was well covered with fat. There were no external marks of violence. The immediate cause of death was evidently syncope, which was obviously, taking into account the mode of death and the changes found after death, not due to disease. I concluded that it must be due to some poison – either alcohol, chloral, or some vegetable alkaloid. All other common poisons could practically be eliminated, and, knowing that chloral had been used by thieves to drug their victims, I determined to have the stomach and intestines analysed for this body. The analyst for the city of Manchester found traces of chloral.

"Several important questions arise in this case. First, was the death due merely to alcohol? Alcohol may cause death in one of three ways: (a) If taken in a very large dose, such as a pint of brandy, drunk off at once, death may result in a very few minutes from shock; (b) when taken in a large total amount, but its administration spread over several hours, it may cause death by syncope preceded by prolonged coma; or (c) the patient, having passed through a comatose stage, may rarely suddenly relapse and die after apparent recovery. Obviously, Mr John Fletcher died in none of these three ways. For death to occur after only such a short period of coma as three-quarters of an hour, as in this case, must be extremely rare. I have seen considerably over two hundred cases of alcoholic coma, but none in which death even threatened within so short a time of the patient becoming comatose, except in two or three cases where large quantities of alcohol had been taken just before coma setting in, which was not the case here. Moreover, to imagine that in a person already only so far poisoned with alcohol that he could walk straight and appear perfectly sober, the administration of the additional amount of alcohol contained in a glass of beer would cause rapid coma and death would appear almost impossible to most medical men, and certainly so to a jury. Lastly, the most constant postmortem sign of acute alcoholic poisoning – namely, a deep cherry-red colour of the gullet, stomach, and intestines – was not present.

"Secondly, would the previous administration of alcohol tend to lessen or to increase the chances of death by syncope from chloral? This is entirely a matter of dosage. A small quantity of alcohol – say an ounce of brandy – is very frequently given with chloral with good effect, as tending to lessen the depressing influence of the latter on the heart. But the case is different with large doses of alcohol previously administered, as here the heart would be much weakened, as evidenced by the very feeble and rapid pulse so commonly seen in cases of alcoholic coma. Whether this cardiac depression from alcohol had occurred in this case before the chloral was administered it is impossible to say, but it is quite probable that this was so.

"As regards the taste of chloral, when dissolved in water, it has a most objectionable pungent, burning taste, which, however, is almost entirely absent when it is taken in beer; all that is perceived being an acrid sensation at the back of the throat, occurring after the beer has been swallowed. When prescribing for the insane, I found that sherry was a most excellent medium for disguising the taste of chloral.

"The dose given in this case is unknown: but it must be remembered that 30 grains are reported to have caused death in a woman and it is always said to be an uncertain drug. Personally, I have always found chloral to be very regular in its action and very safe, having frequently given 30 or 40 grains in a single dose without any bad effects. I have always, however, used it with great care, never giving it when there was feeble cardiac action, or when the patient is very cold.

"The symptoms and *post-mortem* appearances in this case exactly corresponded with all that we know of this drug. The fluidity of the blood found has been before noticed by Richardson, and Dr Dreschfold tells me that it was a marked feature in a case of fatal chloral-poisoning observed by himself. Of course, it is not pathognomonic, but merely one of detail.

"One apparent flaw in this case is the fact that the analyst said he only found a 'trace' of chloral. But it must be remarked that he did not try to estimate the actual amount present, but merely showed its presence by decomposing and obtaining the reactions for chlorine and hydrochloric acid. Now, as he got each of these tests three times, it is, perhaps, hardly accurate to speak of a 'trace.' But taking it for granted for a moment that only a trace was found, this does not in the least alter the arguments in favour of chloral having caused the death; for it must be remembered as a fundamental principle in all analyses of the contents of a stomach in poisoning cases that the portion of poison found in the stomach is only the residue of what has been administered, and is not the actual part which has caused death, this, of course, having been absorbed. This principle is well pointed out by Guy and Ferrier, who state: 'When poison is found in very small quantity, the objection is sure to be advanced that it was not enough to account for death; but to this the reply is obvious that the quantity found must needs fall short of that actually taken ... and that the quantity found in the stomach is only the surplus of what may have been sufficient to cause death by absorption. The discovery, therefore, of a quantity of poison insufficient to destroy life is scarcely even a presumption that the substance was not administered in a poisonous dose.' Woodman and Tidy also state that: 'The discovery of a very small portion in the stomach is no criterion of the quantity taken.' With a body so rapidly absorbed as chloral, this principle is all the more important to remember.

"Finally, all the symptoms, the *post-mortem* examination, and the analysis coincided with the fact that chloral had been administered. Taking this for granted, no one can for a moment doubt that the administration of this body to a man whose heart was already enfeebled with alcohol and slight fatty degeneration most certainly hastened the death if it did not actually cause it. Now, if in this manner death was accelerated even by a single minute, then it is perfectly correct to say that the administrator of the chloral caused the death."

PART FIVE
CHARLES PARTON'S ACCOUNT

CHAPTER XXIII

Introduction

Subsequent to his release from prison, in the mid 1920s, Parton told his side of the story in a pamphlet entitled, *The True Story of the Manchester Cab Mystery, Sentenced To Death At 18 Years Of Age (My Life In Prison)*, price one shilling. The account follows:

CHAPTER XXIV

Charles Parton's Disclosure, Part I

The Manchester Cab mystery was a notorious and mysterious affair, but the truth about it has never been properly made public. Now, for the first time I intend to disclose the real facts of the tragedy. No one is more qualified to do so than myself. I was in the cab with the "murdered" man, and I was afterwards sentenced to death as his murderer.

The curtain rises upon the drama in a street in Manchester late at night. A cab was rattling along the otherwise silent and almost deserted thoroughfare when a stray passer-by noticed in the flickering light from a gas-light, that the door of the vehicle was open and was swinging backwards and forwards.

"Hey!" he called to the driver, "your cab door's open."

Pulling up, the driver dismounted and made to close the door. He was just about to do so when he noticed his fare was lying in the seat with a deathly pallor upon him. He called him, then shook him, but there was no response. The man was dead. The driver immediately got in touch with the police.

Jerome Caminada, the celebrated Manchester detective, took up the threads of the case, which was to bring him greater fame and glory than ever – at the expense of an innocent man.

The first suspicion of foul play arose when the cabman related that there had been another passenger in the cab, a youth of eighteen, but there had been no sign of him when the driver stopped. The police then made the discovery that the dead man, who was soon identified as a rich paper manufacturer named John Fletcher, Justice of the Peace and Town Councillor, had been robbed of money and a watch and chain valued at a hundred guineas. Further, a *post-mortem* showed that some sort of drug had been administered to him.

At this time cases of drugging for the purposes of robbery were frequent in Manchester and they were causing considerable alarm in the public's mind. Murder as well could have increased their concern still further. Jerome Caminada thus made up his mind that he would find the killer at all costs. The detective arrested hundreds of suspected criminals, and when, nine days after the discovery of the mystery, I was arrested and taken to the Town Hall, where the suspects were quartered, I found the place packed to the doors. I myself recognized at least fifty crooks with whom I had associated.

Had it not been so tragic, it would have been laughable when, upon my arrival, there was a chorus of, "What, got you too, have they?" from scores of notorious characters.

But, give credit where credit is due. This time they had got hold of the right man.

I admit I robbed John Fletcher, not of five pounds and a watch, as the police suggested at the time, but of £500 in addition to the timepiece. But I did not murder him. I know that most criminals protest their innocence, just as I am doing, even after they have been convicted by damming evidence. But in my case my innocence was proved. Medical testimony was eventually forthcoming to show that the man I robbed had died, not of poison, but of heart failure. It took eleven years to establish that fact to the satisfaction of the authorities, and for most of those eleven years I was languishing in solitary confinement to pay for the crime.

Eleven years of torture! No one knows the agony, the utterable anguish I endured, first in the shadow of the gallows, then wearing out the years behind those cold grey walls. They say that condemned men get anything they want to eat while waiting to be hanged. It is not true. I was half-starved as I lay under sentence. Even after the reprieve, it was three years before I was granted the privilege and luxury of a cup of tea. And I shall have a tale to tell of other sufferings.

But before dealing, among other things, with my emotions as I waited for the day when I should be led from my cell and hanged, let me detail the inner history of the cab mystery. As I have indicated, I was only eighteen years of age at the time.

Like my father, I was something of a boxer, and my enthusiasm for sport led me to horse-racing, which was the beginning of my downfall. I became associated in Manchester with a racing gang in which were a number of known thieves, some of whom had already done penal servitude.

One day, I was walking along Deansgate when I met some of those "boys." With them was John Fletcher, and the members of the clique signalled me to join them, one of them whispering that the old man had a lot of money on him. We went to a public house, where glasses of beer were ordered. While Fletcher's attention was diverted, one of the gang placed some chloral hydrate in his drink. This drug is a sedative, and was used then as extensively as aspirin is now to relieve nerve pains. The amount put in the glass was afterwards found to be thirty grains.

The drink was passed over to Fletcher and he took a sip of it. That was all he had, for the glass was upset. But it was enough.

He began to get restless, and I suggested he should leave with me. He agreed, and I gave my confederates the wink that I would finish the business. Outside we hailed a cab, and I told the driver to go to the first address in Oxford Road that came to my mind. Fletcher himself did not know where he wanted to go, as by now the drink and the drug had thoroughly muddled his wits. We got in, and the cab had not proceeded far before I was searching through my companion's pockets. He tried to push me off, but his resistance was too feeble to do any good. I secured the notes, removed his watch and got out of the cab while it was still in motion. The next moment the dark had swallowed me up.

When I jumped from the cab Fletcher was alive and unhurt. I used no violence whatever and had no doubt that the man would be fine and well by the following day. Little could I have known that, a few moments later, he would be dead.

Having placed me under lock and key, Caminada sought to get me to incriminate myself. To do this he induced a friend of my father's to carry out a bit of treachery. This man, who was also acquainted with the dead man's family, came to me and talked through the cell grating, imploring me to say where the watch was, as it was a family heirloom. Foolishly I told him what he wanted to hear.

These words were my death warrant. Caminada had been standing behind my "friend" and had heard the fateful admission of my guilt. I was charged and, soon enough, I appeared at trial.

The evidence against me was purely circumstantial. I had not, of course, revealed the names of the accomplices with whom I had shared the proceeds of the robbery, so they were safe. But every word I told the court was the truth. The judge, addressing the jury before they retired to consider whether they should grant me life or death, said, "I am convinced in my own mind, and I think you will agree with me, that the prisoner at the bar had no intention of taking the deceased's life. His intentions were to stupefy for the purpose of robbery. But if you bring this mere boy in guilty of this charge, I have no alternative but to sentence him to death – the most painful duty I will have ever experienced in my whole career."

The judge then went on to stress what he described as a scandal in the law of England. If I had been tried in Scotland or America, he said, I should have been tried for manslaughter on the evidence. But English law lays it down that where a man kills another, unintentionally or otherwise, and the crime is accompanied by robbery, he must be charged with murder. That law, glaring in its injustice, is still on the Statute Book.

There was an awesome hush in the court when the jury retired. During the trial I had maintained my composure, even smiling sometimes, although the ordeal was such a terrible one. No one can imagine what ghastly horror fills the mind of a man who stands in the dock with his life at stake. Grave of face, the jury men returned. The foreman rose to his feet. My heart seemed to stop beating.

"We find the prisoner guilty," he said, in a low voice, "but strongly recommend him to mercy."

The judge passed sentence of death upon me, and said he would see that the recommendation reached the proper quarters, and that it would be endorsed and supported by himself. I swayed and my brain reeled. For a minute or so it seemed that I must be dreaming. Two warders took me by the arms and I was led down the steps and out into a waiting cab. The trial had taken place at the Liverpool Assizes, and I was conveyed to Kirkdale Prison and placed in the condemned cell.

Night and day there was a warder with me, three of them taking it in turns to watch me until I should be handed over to the executioner. They seemed to me to be inhuman ghouls as they watched my every move. Now, when I look back and think of the conditions and circumstances in which they were going to send me to my doom, my blood boils.

For breakfast I had 8 oz of bread and a pint of porridge, and the same in the evening, and usually bully beef, bad potatoes, and bread at midday. We had pudding and soup three times a week. That wouldn't have been so bad if there had been enough, but being a healthy lad I had a big appetite, and was almost starving with the meagre fare.

Most of all I longed for a cup of tea. One day an official from the Home Office called to ask if I had any last request. "Yes," I replied, "Give me a cup of tea!" After a lot of trouble and fuss my request was granted.

I broke down only once in the condemned cell. My mother and father, brothers and sister, came to say good bye. The parting took place in a room divided into two by iron bars. I was on one side of the room, my loved ones on the other. In the middle and between us was a passage-way with iron bars on both sides, and up and down this a warder walked to make sure we did not try to shake hands. Two other warders were there to make sure no signs were passed.

I was not even allowed a farewell kiss from my mother. All I could do was to stand in my blue prison clothes and read the misery of my dear ones. When the interview, which lasted only a few minutes, was over and I was led away, my tiny sister called out, "This way, Charlie," and pointed to the door they had come in by. She thought I was at liberty to go with them, not knowing my life was forfeit.

The warders who watched over me night and day in the condemned cell tried to cheer me up the best they could, but what alleviation could there be from the thought ever in my mind that each day brought me nearer to the scaffold?

Time seemed to move incredibly swiftly. The day fixed for my death was about three weeks from the date of sentence. They still kept me on the fourth-class diet allowed under prison regulations. This was to me, a strong healthy youth of eighteen, practically starvation rations. I was hungry all the time.

The fourth day from the date fixed for my execution I was sitting talking to the warder on guard when the Chief Warder appeared. In his hand he held a sheet of official looking paper.

"Well, Parton," he said, "they've let you off."

My first emotion was of such intense relief that I almost broke down, but on top of that came the thought – I had been spared from the gallows, but the rest of my life would be spent within these grim walls. With the awful possibilities that this conjured up, my feelings changed.

I told myself I would prefer the momentary pang of the hangman's noose to the life-long misery of penal servitude. I had heard more than sufficient from my old associates to decide that death was preferable.

CHAPTER XXV

Charles Parton's Disclosure, Part II

Parton's account continued.

They took me from the condemned cell and exchanged the blue suit for the drab garb of the ordinary convict. For three weeks I was detained in Kirkdale Prison at Liverpool then I was removed to Stafford Jail. Here began another phase of the living martyrdom to which I was subjected. For nine months I was the victim of the "Silent System." This was the name given to the solitary confinement regulations for penal servitude men. I was placed in a cell from which I was allowed out only one hour in twenty-four. During the other twenty-three hours I was alone, deprived even of the solace of books with which to keep my mind from becoming unhinged. The only break was when the warders came with my food. During the day I was kept at work making slippers.

For the first six months I was not allowed to have letters. Nor was I permitted to receive visitors. In due course I was removed to Portland. With 22 other convicts all chained together, I was placed in the luggage-van of the train and taken to Portland, where I was set to work in the quarries.

At the beginning conditions here were somewhat easy. But the time came when this comparative leniency gave way to a veritable reign of terror. Convicts who were insufficiently fed were given almost superhuman tasks to accomplish, such as filling so many trucks a day. Men were driven to such desperate straits that some put their arms under the truck wheels so that they were amputated and the victims could do no more manual labour. The system, however, was equal to them. For such men was introduced the mule-gang; halters were placed round their necks and they had to draw loaded trucks as if they were animals.

Within three months even those prisoners who had been notable for good conduct over periods of years were undergoing some punishment or other.

The prison governor died shortly after I arrived. On his death-bed he requested both the chaplains – Catholic and Protestant – to tell the prisoners that he had tried to do his duty, and if he had harmed any of us he had done so unintentionally, and he asked for our pardon and prayers. The following Sunday those old lags, whose hearts one would have imagined to have become long since hardened and unresponsive to sentiment, prayed for the dead governor with unashamed earnestness.

Another source of torture at Portland was the chain gang. Convicts reported for bad conduct were submitted to this harshness. Round each ankle an iron clamp was riveted by the prison blacksmith, and to these clamps chains were attached which extended up the legs to the waist, where they were fixed to a body-belt. Night and day for six months, working, eating, or sleeping, the prisoner had to wear these chains, which all the while rasped the skin.

I was never sentenced to the chain-gang, but my plight was bad enough. The cell in which I was placed, and where I remained for nine years, provided sufficient torture in itself. It was seven feet high, six feet long and three feet wide. A man over six feet in height was unable to lie down in it. There was no window. The only illumination, which feebly flickered through the cell-door grating, came from a door at the end of the corridor. Certainly cells on the outside had windows, but one had to wait one's turn for them. In nine years my turn never came.

During the winter I would be out at work in the quarries until darkness came on. We would then be returned to our cells, where everything was pitch-dark. There was not even a candle.

Some of the convicts went mad in the Portland nightmare. Others became quite irresponsible in their light-headedness. They would stare to their feet in chapel and begin mumbling to themselves. In chapel one was not even allowed to turn one's head, let alone speak.

I was in Portland at the same time as John Lee, "the man they could not hang." I considered him to be a much inferior individual to most of my other companions. Lee had been sentenced for the murder of an old lady who had befriended him and his sister. He was placed three times on the scaffold and each time the drop refused to act. When Lee got off the scaffold the second time, a bag of potatoes was placed in position and the trap gave way as it should have done with Lee. But when Lee returned, the trap stayed shut yet again. Following the third and final attempt to hang the condemned man, a warder stepped on to the drop holding a rope attached to the gallows. The drop immediately gave way beneath him. Most people, particularly superstitious folks, regarded Lee's escape as a sign from Providence of his innocence of the murder. This belief was strengthened when it was declared that on her deathbed Lee's sister had stated she and not her brother had killed their benefactress.

This information was conveyed to the Home Secretary, who then got in touch with the prison chaplain. In the course of the official investigation that followed, the chaplain was informed of the sister's statement. "Oh," replied the chaplain, "this man has already confessed to me." The sister apparently made up the confession to get her brother released. Lee remained in prison for 23 years.

Another of my prison acquaintances was that notorious swindler and robber of the poor, Jabez Balfour. I also associated with a Peer of the Realm who had been sentenced to five years penal servitude for forging his aunt's name. He went back again later in connection with the theft of some jewellery.

After the terrors of Portland I was glad to be removed to Dartmoor. Before leaving the very sore question of my treatment at Portland, I should like to mention that, although I was a Catholic, never once during the whole of the nine years did a priest visit me.

Captain Johnson was governor at Dartmoor, and Captain Sir Basil Thompson was his deputy. Sir Basil was well liked by all the men. He was very humane. If there had been only a few more prison governors like him there would never have been the same number of criminals turned out from the prisons, which for the most part were nothing but training grounds for malefactors.

I remained in Dartmoor for two years, which made eleven years imprisonment in all. During all this time my mother had been working hard organizing a petition. She employed people to go around the country – she spent all her small fortune in this way – to get people's signatures. By this time too, the medical aspects of the case had been thoroughly thrashed out in the columns of the medical journals. The Public Analyst of Leicester stated that the amount of drug placed in the dead man's drink – 30 grains – was insufficient to kill a baby. The dead man, too, had taken only a small sip. The analyst added his complete belief that the deceased's heart was in such a condition that he would have died that night in any case, even if I had never met him and taken him upon that fateful ride in the cab.

My mother's petition, combined with this revelation, resulted in my release. I had served eleven years for a murder I had not committed. In spite of that, however, I was not pardoned. I was released on a "ticket-of-leave," the only life sentence man ever discharged under twelve years. The ticket-of-leave meant that at any time I could be taken away again for the term of my natural life. If I even led an "idle life" this was what would happen to me.

Next I shall expose the evils of this iniquitous system which deprived me even of the right to choose my own religion. Since my release I have been "sent back" to terms totalling nearly ten years, and all for trivial offences.

On the ticket-of-leave card given to me when I passed through the gates of Dartmoor Prison there are some astonishing conditions under which I enjoy my so-called freedom. It is laid down that I must not "lead an idle and dissolute life, without visible means of obtaining an honest livelihood." Once every month I must report to the police, and if I stir beyond the district in which I reside I must give the authorities a reason for my movements. I am prohibited from being found in or upon any dwelling-house, or any building, yard or premises being parcel of or attached to such dwelling house, or in or upon any shop, warehouse, counting-house, or other place of business, or in any garden or orchard, pleasure ground, and so on, without being able to account to the satisfaction of the court for my being there.

These are only a few of the regulations under which I am allowed to exist. If I do not observe them I am liable to undergo penal servitude for life. Imagine it! If I am found sitting in a public park and I am unable to prove that quiet enjoyment is my sole reason for being there, I can be sent to prison again, to remain there until death gives me release. The ticket-of-leave man is thus no better than a hounded dog. I have said that my soul is not my own, and I mean it.

I was only eighteen years of age when I was sentenced. Eleven years afterwards I was free again. Surrounded on all sides by the fetters under which I received my licence, I decided it would be better for me if I left the country and tried to start again. Without notifying the authorities I went to Canada. That to begin with was an offence which could have made my liberty forfeit. But what other chance did I have? What other way could I have lived a life?

After wanderings in Canada, South Africa and New Zealand, I eventually settled down in the Argentine, where I set up a business. I tried to live down the past. My business, a café, prospered, and everything was going splendidly. But then the war broke out.

I returned to enlist – and once more brought myself within the reach of the law. Under the name of Charles Mack I joined the 10th Devons, and for training we went to Bath where I met the woman who is now my wife and the mother of my children. She herself had had a tragic life. I told her my story and we agreed to get married. We have never regretted it, although we have since often been separated by prison walls.

To cut a long story short, the time came when I once more found myself pursued by the police. A Manchester man in my regiment recognized me and, fearing arrest for failing to notify my movements, I fled. I had no intention of deserting for I still wanted to serve my country. But how could I have served it behind bars? I resolved to join another regiment and this is exactly what I did.

Three days later I joined the 4th East Surreys. I gave a different name, as a result of which my wife could draw the allowance. It had already been stopped by my first regiment.

My family was soon in want, and in desperation I stole a bag at Euston Station. I was arrested. I do not complain about that, nor about my sentence of six months. What I do protest against is that, as I offended as a ticket-of-leave man, I was sent back, after completing six months, to an 'indefinite period' in Portland. Can you imagine the mental agony of that? I did not know whether I was in for a year or until I died! Outside, my wife and children were left to starve.

After three years I was slowly dying. The prison doctor could find nothing wrong with me and another medical man was called in. "Have you anything on your mind?" this doctor asked, when he also discovered no physical ailment. Anything on my mind!

They heard my story and passed it on to the authorities. As a result they took compassion on me. They allowed me out. Finally, nearly four years after I stole that bag, I was free once again.

In Scotland they are more humane. There, a life-sentence man is released after twenty years. He is out on ticket, but after seven years the licence expires and the man is really free. Why can we not do the same in England and not hound a man on licence until he dies? "You must not lead an idle life," my ticket says. How could I lead an honest one? If I approached an employer I had to produce my licence and tell him I was a ticket-of-leave man. Otherwise the police could arrest me again. With thousands of honest men available to get work, what hope for a man who has been convicted of murder?

A local magistrate, before whom I was brought for hawking balloons, asked me, "Why don't you get some regular employment?"

"Are you prepared to give me regular employment?" I asked him. "Would you be willing to have me behind your counter, handling your money, knowing the stigma attached to my name?"

I am lucky now in having solved the problem of employment. I earn an honest living by going round the country selling printed copies of the very licence which brought all this misery upon me.

This system reminds me of medieval torture. Hugo wrote of the martyrdom of Jean Valjean in the penitentiaries of France. There are Jean Valjeans alive in this country today in the persons of ticket-of-leave men who after years of living death, are set "free" from prison. With every hand against them, is it surprising that in time many of them come to be haters of the world and enemies of society?

It seems there is no one in this civilised land who has either the power, or the sympathy, to put a stop to this distorted conception of justice.